love
connection

Lesa Childress
&Jamie Ward

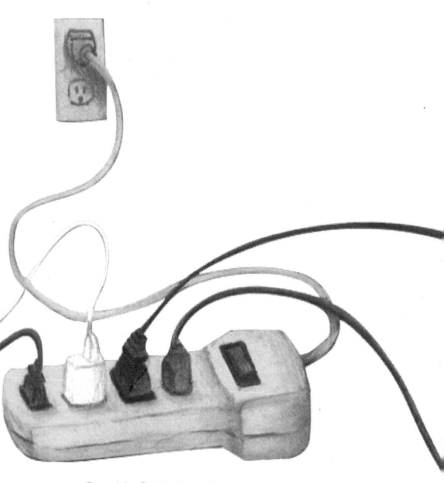

ISBN-10: 0615849776
ISBN-13:9780615849775

Dedication

Jamie

To all the baby chickens and mama birds that desire them. To my groom who wanted a family even more truly than I did and gives our chickens a strong heritage and a godly example for them to follow.

Lesa

To all the women who will encounter a choice and to all the men and women who will receive a promise because of this choice.

To my English teacher, Michael Borich and his wife Lynn, who believed in me and spoke to my God potential—because of your encouragement this book was written.

...and to the three best friends that anyone could ever have.

contents

acknowledgments

First off, we want to recognize the One who gave us this story to share. If it wasn't for Our God than this book wouldn't have been possible. With Jesus and the Holy Spirit by our side we were able to finish with love, support and guidance throughout.

Secondly, we would like to thank everyone that came together on our behalf, who put their time and effort into this novel—expecting nothing in return—helping us as servants of Christ. It was an honor to work with those who truly understand what it is to be a disciple of the Most High and who continually use their gifts to honor Him in all the ways that they can.

Tammy Hammonds Patrick came to our aid by editing--sacrificing countless hours that she could have spent elsewhere. No words can describe the gratitude we have toward this woman! Thank you!

Jeff Rawson designed the front and back cover. Although, He had many other paying clients, he humbled himself and helped us out. His artwork and talents were used in obedience to God and We were blown away by how perfect it all was!

Brandon Hallock designed the interior of our book. We cannot thank him enough as he did this through sacrifice and love. He is also expecting a baby boy and in the midst of preparing for his upcoming future, he took the time to help us at the spur of the moment and quickly replied until all our needs were met. His reliability will always stick out to us as well as his dependability.

Matt Richards created a phenomenal promo video for our book. We are grateful that he took the time and effort to shoot, create, and edit our video to make a professional video that we could use to get the word out there! His talents continue to amaze me!

To all Lesa's family and Jamie's family and friends for adding to our story—their accounts—and for being willing to be used by God to create a story that will inspire many to come!

All of these lovely people went above and beyond, carrying us not only one mile but two, and for that…

we   are   humbled   and   graciously   thankful.

i

PROLOGUE

"I'd throw myself on the mercy of God. After all, He's famous for great and unexpected acts; there's no end to His surprises." JOB 5:9 MSG

Laughter in the street below fluttered into the heightened loft windows and faded into a distant murmur as it reached my ears. As the sun lowered in the sky, it was clear that the downtown party had just begun. The clinking of beer bottles, the yelling of pre-drunk maniacs, the sound of jewelry jingling, and the hammering of heels on the pavement echoed in all directions.

Next to me, a lighter flickered. I watched as a flame began to rise beneath a glass pipe that held my escape. The turn was soon mine to melt down my mind's barriers and smoke what I believed made me sane. I looked into the hourglass of delusions where the sands of time defied gravity. I inhaled deep breaths of schizophrenic paranoia and exhaled all judgment when the flame burned out. "Want another hit, Lesa?" Chase asked with strung-out eagerness. Shaking my head back and forth, I indicated doubtfully that I had enough.

Both of us knew however, that enough was never enough.

We wandered into the bedroom where our dilated pupils met in agreement. Surrendering my body to his, we descended into the silky sheets, the only place we could define our relationship. Never having to wonder if the love was real when my conscious mind was submerged, I kept defending the relationship that had always been on edge, teeter-tottering on the cliff of disastrous heartbreak. For a moment, it was as if we had flown away to our own never-land.

The violent strike of reality had a potent sting when the initial gratification was through. As he rolled over, high to the point of exhaustion, Chase's eyes rolled to the back of his head. He had passed out leaving me to face arising thoughts on my own. I reflected over the past five months. I realized I was patient with Chase who had brought me into this surreal place. But he was always in a mood that would snap hard one way or another; I never knew what to expect. No matter how bad things turned out, the excitement of the unknown kept me from walking away.

The fights were physical. If things didn't go his way he would yell at me, choke me, burn me with cigarettes, or even pour the alcoholic beverage he was drinking onto me. How did I think I was happy in the midst of all this? Holding strongly to the few times he would make me smile made it me think it was all worth it. Who did I have if I didn't have him?

The truth that I rejected in my inebriation was it hadn't ever been my Never-land. I was living in his and it's hard to live in a world that doesn't belong to you. The only way to be happy would be to please the one who owned it. Not caring about my own well-being, this had been the life I held onto. The only life I felt I had ever known.

I stared at the ceiling and then gathered my tingling body up to make my way back into the room where we had started our promiscuous adventure. As I grabbed for the pipe that still held my desire, I lit up; I began to nimbly twirl the glass between my fingers and lightly breathed away the somatic sensation of discomfort that had started to catch up with my defeated mind.

Although I was alone, whispers filled the shadows. The sun peeked through the blinds that had been lowered and shut to prevent the concerns of the world from spilling in. As the light reached into the gaps of every slat of plastic, it grabbed me by surprise.

A groaning from the other side of the thinned-brick loft wall kept me aware of Chase's presence. I contemplated the fact that it had been another sleepless night for me. Had it been three days? Or even a week since I had slept? Trying to decide what the outcome would be of his drug-induced slumber, I mulled over if he would remember the closeness that we had shared only hours before or if he would be furious that I had not stayed in the bed curled up beside him and then drown me in accusations of being unfaithful.

Creaky wooden floorboards harbored the exaggerated stomp of heavy feet. As the creaking had increased in intensity, so did my insecurity. I averted my eyes to the floor where Chase would soon be standing and prepared myself for it to become the all-too-familiar battle ground.

A feeble, translucent face covered in rough lines

of agitation and an indefinite number of scars from a confined experience, appeared in the doorway. I remembered when that once healthy, glowing face would look at me with eyes of adoration. Where his eyes had previously conveyed enthusiastic excitement—now gleamed rampant. His cracked lips tightened. Adjusting to the light that now entered the room; he fixed his stare from me onto the pipe that held a notably smaller amount. Biting his lower lip, he started to scowl "Who was here?" He questioned irrevocably. "Just me." I answered quietly. Repressed rage turned his face scarlet as he slowly turned from me and went back into the bedroom.

A dissonant sound clamored and then quickly began to proceed in my direction. A dresser drawer is all I saw before the quick opening of blinds and a flick of hands. In a fluid motion, Chase had happened to run past me with the dresser drawer that held all my belongings, what little I had, and he dumped everything out onto the pavement below. Shocked, I stared. Anger burned in my heart. He smiled smugly walking past me; I jumped up and grabbed him by his ears, pounding my fists as hard as I could on his back, chest, and face. I couldn't stop. I wanted to kill him. Screaming, I was thrown off his back and onto the floor. He laughed because he knew what control he had over me. I had nowhere else to go. If I left here, I would be back in my car. He certainly knew how to finish the game, almost too easily, his lips spoke two words that we both knew would eventually come…the two words that in the end, would release me from my prison… "Get out."

"So, what a blessing when God steps in, mind you! Don't despise the discipline of Almighty God! True, He wounds, but He also dresses the wound; the same hand that hurts you, heals you. From one disaster after another He delivers you; no matter what the calamity, the evil can't touch you--" Job 5:17-19 MSG

Do you feel like you have gone from valley to valley--hurt, depressed, unconfident, confused, angry, bitter, attempted suicide, or succumbed to an addiction with no apparent way out? Sometimes things seem to go from bad to worse in just a matter of months, days, or even hours. We wonder why the enemy is attacking us so hard or why God is letting this happen! Yes, by enemy, I refer to the enemy of our souls, Satan. Sometimes, it may seem as though the situation we are facing goes from difficult to impossible.

What calamity or disaster are you currently facing?
Does it seem difficult or impossible to come out of?
Have you looked for help or are you trying to face these challenges on your own?
Do you feel like you are being attacked in every aspect of your life?

When you feel discouraged, depressed, irritated, doubtful, or fearful - it is important to realize that the enemy is getting scared and trying his hardest to keep you right where you are. Don't let the difficult circumstances paralyze you. God is working behind the scenes so He can do a miracle in your life. You may seem stuck but I promise if you keep on moving and chasing after God than you will see Him. He will come through for you. Your situation may have gone from difficult to impossible because God knows you can handle difficult, but He wants you to trust HIM to do the impossible. Nothing can stop Him from conquering evil. All must bow at the presence of our King.

Genesis 37; Genesis 39-41

Joseph was promised things through God-given dreams. Though his hope was to receive God's promise - God had to refine some things in Joseph. He went from being a hopeful young boy with the "perfect" platform to receive God's promises to being stripped and discouraged, without any explanation for the circumstances he was abruptly put in.

Nowhere in scripture is it documented that Joseph became bitter. He lived in his circumstances and was favored. Joseph always credited his victories and abilities to God. Though he was placed in slavery unjustly, abused and abandoned by family that was supposed to protect him and then thrown into jail without warrant of any guilt, God was with him, showed him favor and eventually gave him a way out. Because of his journey, Joseph's character was fully formed to accept his position completely as the Pharaoh's second in command, in charge of all of Egypt. (Genesis 41:43).

At the end of all of it Joseph was able to face the very ones that hurt him and say, "You intended to harm me, but God intended it all for good. He brought me to this position so I could save the lives of many people." (Genesis 50:20NLT)

We believe God wants you to be able to say at the completion of your impossible situation that "God causes everything to work together for the good of those who love Him and are called according to His purpose for them." (Romans 8:28NLT)

Be encouraged, lovely one - God always has a purpose for your journey & the impossible circumstances in your life. God always stacks the odds against Himself to show He is the only way out. And we believe it is always for the benefit of advancing His kingdom - "for the saving of many lives." (Genesis 50:20 NIV)

We all have a story - a complicated, hard and even impossible story. God is always able and wants to use your life in His story. That He will be made known and that others are drawn to Him and are encouraged in the faith of our Lord Jesus Christ.

June

"You have put me in the depths of the pit, in the regions dark and deep." PSALM 88:6 ESV

Adapting to the environment, my car harbored the scent of spilt liquor and peppermint cloves. I nestled my head on a thin tightly-knit sweater. Clothes were scattered everywhere, serving more as a covering to my floorboards than to my own emaciated body. My eyes, heavy as if they took the stinging burden of hatred from my heart and carried it on their lids, fell captive to the weight and I quickly dozed off.

Discontent, I woke and thrust away the once-white towel I was covered with and climbed into the driver's seat. I hastily shuffled around for my keys and found them tucked away under a water bottle. Anxiously, placing the key into the ignition, a deep prolonged cry brought it to a start. The gas light flashed red and the small pin that fell below the "E" from my fuel gauge exasperated me.

I knew I could stay in the parking lot and drive myself mad staring at the door to Chase's loft or I could try to get to the one place I knew I could drown my hostility. Chase had introduced me to his drug dealer and secretly I had been texting him. His name was Stephen and I knew that he would take me in and provide me with my mental escape. Slowly, I took in one last breath filled with envy, turned my back and dolefully drove away.

Rejection injected itself through my veins. A wall of lies had been constructed in my mind, effectively shutting out the truth. I had believed I was worthless, with no purpose for living, a thief, a slut, and that I deserved nothing. These beliefs caused me to find myself at the mercy of the man in charge of dealing the drugs I cherished and that satisfied the craving that still held me close.

As I pulled up to the simplistic townhouse that appeared as any ordinary home, the security cameras reminded me otherwise. Paranoia was reflected in every lens. Two cars sat side by side in the driveway, a vast variety of car parts littered the ground beneath, confirming Stephen was home. Both cars belonged to Stephen who had a fond affection for mechanics and "fixing up" broken technology. However, the projects never seemed to come to an end. If there was nothing to fix, he would create something to fix, taking things apart just to put them back together.

The doorbell did not work, so I knew that I would have to knock quietly. If I knocked too hard, he might think I was a cop and I did not want to cause any harm to either of us. I contemplated to myself that I just needed someone to take me in. I found my hope in Stephen. A worn out willowy figure showed up in the doorway. I assumed it had been a few sunsets since he had last slept. A smile crept across his face as he welcomed me in.

We passed through the living room and I noticed a trail of toys, books, and a little pair of pink socks, leading through the hallway and into the back room. My curiosity went ahead of me as we stopped at his room a few feet away from where the trail ended. "That's my daughter's room," Stephen said in response to the puzzled look on my face. "Oh," I said aloud. My brain was trying to make sense of the situation.

Irritation consumed me because all I had wanted to do was get high. I was worried that his daughter would ruin my expectations because she would want to play and talk to me. When I was high all I wanted to do was float away and not be bothered; I enjoyed being left alone. "She's with her mom and won't be back for about a week." He assured me softly. Stephen took my hand and escorted me to his bed. I couldn't wait for what came next. He reached over me to his bedside table and grabbed a glass pipe hidden under a pile of cords and old broken phones. We lit up and melted into the pillows. At that moment, we found sheer satisfaction.

Deeper and deeper I went, further and further I buried myself in the bottomless well of my desire, letting my mind slip away for days into the fictional world where nothing mattered, all my emotions became entwined into one. What was this emotion, though? Was it joy, happiness, or something else altogether? I didn't know; all seemed foreign to me. Always craving and wanting more and more while never getting enough, that's what I knew. I knew the feeling of defeat and I was getting exhausted.

Ready to just give up, I realized the true emptiness that my life had become. I had no motivation to change, just to quit digging. I put down the shovel, stopped going deeper, refused to climb out, and just laid there. That's when I collapsed back into reality. Nothing could get me high the way I wanted. What else was there?

Stephen started to notice my change in mood and appetite. "You haven't eaten in days, are you sure you aren't hungry?" He questioned. "I'm not hungry." I assured as my stomach's loud grumbles claimed otherwise. "Well, I am going to make a pizza. You can eat some if you want." He sympathized as he stood up and peered down at the scrawny mess of me. Politely I smiled and thanked him. He took good care of me. He watched out for me. I was a wreck but from what I could tell, I began to have feelings for him.

He waltzed back in with a whole sliced up pizza. Rapidly, he set it down on the end of the bed and then left again to grab some napkins. I couldn't take my eyes off the pizza. I reached for a slice only to find that it was extremely hot! As I pulled my hand away, Stephen walked back in and chuckled. "I could have warned you it was hot, but I thought you weren't hungry," He jested as he picked up a piece and handed it to me. "I am never hungry when I smoke this stuff," I admitted, "but I am about ready to eat this whole thing."

Why was it so good? I had never enjoyed food so much! After eating about 5 slices, Stephen made a funny face as he watched me scarf down the remaining pepperoni that had fallen onto my lap. "You're eating like you're pregnant or something!" he exclaimed jokingly.

Paranoia hit me like a sack of rocks. I realized that I was gaining weight in spite of my malnutrition. I also couldn't remember the last time I had my menstrual cycle. My face dropped and Stephen became concerned. "I was just messing around with you, but if that could be something you're worried about, I have tests under my sink. You can take one if you want." He quizzically studied my face as I agreed. Like a fire was lit under me, I jumped from under the covers and raced to the bathroom; My heart raced along with me! I convinced myself this couldn't be happening.

Three minutes later, we had the results. A small red plus sign presented itself. Continually, I bit my lip and displayed it to Stephen with anticipation that he would know what to say. Impatience parted my lips before he even had a chance to react. "I'm not mad. I actually don't care. Now I just have a problem that needs fixed." I claimed as my grip tightened on the pregnancy test. "Clinics are expensive. Let me know if you need my help. I am here for you." Stephen concluded and then added, "I know a few friends that have had abortions done. You're going to want to do it as soon as possible, but I want you to think about your options."

Promptly, I requested that Stephen provide me with answers, I questioned his knowledge. "Where do I go? Where do I start? How much is the procedure? Is it going to hurt?" The inquiries went on for days and after about a week, Stephen seemed uninterested.

Not getting anywhere, confusion, followed by loneliness, blanketed me like a fog over a deserted road. Blinded by this emotional fog, I pursued online sites I assumed would lead me to the exact clinic I needed to rid of the 'thing' that was growing inside me. After a week of seeking on my own, day in and day out, I got discouraged. The only thing I wanted to do was get high and stop thinking. If Stephen wasn't going to be there for me, I needed to go somewhere that I would be taken more seriously. I slipped into some blue jeans and a t-shirt, grabbed my keys and said a silent good-bye. If Stephen wasn't going to help me then I would find someone who would.

I dialed my sister because I believed she would provide me with some sort of insight. I didn't tell her the news over the phone. Following two hours of driving and two sleepless days, I pulled up to my sister's quaint little duplex tucked away in a small town

outside of the city. My sister met me outside at my car and handed me a cigarette. "It's good to see you." She said smiling while lighting my cigarette. "Thanks for inviting me. It's good to see you too. I can't wait to just relax and get away from all the drama" I sputtered as I let the smoke pour from behind my lips. "So, what is it you have to tell me?" She tapped ashes and looked at me quizzically. "Let's talk inside." I insisted.

My sister was smart and possessed an indescribable talent. She had a way of looking at situations and turning the negative into positive. She could make you feel better when the rest of the world told you that you had made a huge mistake from which there is no recovery. I entered the house and wanted to just crash. It was nice to be somewhere I felt I belonged. The fresh scent of cookies solidified the warm welcome. Nervously, I walked into the living room and sat, dreading the conversation where I would not only have to say out loud that I was pregnant, but I would actually have to believe it.

KAYLA

That morning started out like any other at my house, feeding the kids, cleaning and doing other household chores. When I looked at my phone and saw my sister's name I was a little surprised. Since I moved, we rarely spoke or saw each other. Really, it had been that way since I was sixteen and moved out of my parents' house pregnant with my first child. Our lives had just drifted in different directions. Little did I know when I accepted that call that our lives would change forever.

"Hey there," I answered happily. "Hey what's up? Can I come over? I'm on my way and I have something to tell you," she replied directly. "Yeah, of course, see you shortly." I hung up the phone and sat down. I had heard that tone in her voice before and knew in my heart what she had to tell me. I knew because at one point, I had said those same words, in the same tone. I waited and prayed that I was wrong.

As soon as she pulled up, I walked outside to meet her. I noticed she looked thin, but it had been awhile, so maybe I was just imagining it. She followed me into the house where my boyfriend, Charles, was now up and preparing to play his video games. They greeted one another and we sat down on the couch.

At first we chatted about small things such as our little brother, work, school, parents, anything to avoid why she was really here. Finally though, the time had come to face it. "So what did you need to tell me?" I asked mentally preparing myself for her response. "I'm pregnant," she said, her eyes faced the ground. Silently, I reeled. Why? Why did this happen to her? She has no

idea what this even means! I didn't want my response to be cold but I knew there were only two options. She looked up at me and met my gaze. "Abortion or adoption?" I asked to relay to her exactly what I had secretly been thinking.

Rosa

The weekend ended too soon and I had yet to face the tough decisions ahead of me. However, it was back to reality and I couldn't face it on my own. I wasn't ready to go back to Stephen's; he had really not been of any help. I knew I had to go back to the place I ran from to confront the fears that had been growing since the day I found out about my pregnancy. I came to the conclusion that I was going to have to go home that evening.

An all too familiar house stood before me as I pulled into the short, steep, uphill driveway. The very house I had abandoned hadn't changed one shutter. This made it even harder; the broken memories had stayed stuck right in the cracks of those brick walls. Last time I was here, I fought with my family, I was a broken mess; now, here I was coming back more broken than the stories the house held.

Exhausted, I took in a few deep breaths. I braced myself for breaking the news to my mom. I didn't know how she would take it. One part of me was thinking of my sister who had also gotten pregnant, moved out, and was now raising a little girl while trying to keep her life from falling apart. The other part of me was thinking of the one way to rid myself of the same fate and not make my mother endure what she did with my sister. My perception was once you had a baby, there was no living your life anymore, there was nothing good; everything would be a disaster and it would be the end of me. I thought that having a baby before I was ready was the equivalent of prison or even death.

I opened the obnoxiously thunderous garage door and quickly slid into the house and hoped my mom wouldn't hear me. I lucked out. She was in the bath and wasn't getting out to see who it was. I hadn't run into my little brother yet either. Perfect. I ran and jumped onto the sofa facing the TV and put my feet up. I hated confrontation. As a matter of fact, I had never been good at talking about my feelings without getting really defensive or upset. Noisily, I reached behind me and pulled out a blanket that had been tucked away under tan throw pillows. I wrapped it around me so only my hands and eyes were visible. The sound of the bath draining kept me alert.

Impatiently, I waited for the conversation-- moments away from happening--I tightened my grip on my blanket. I had been sweating, but I refused to ditch the blanket. My mother kept her house at a roaring 80 degrees and I didn't have the courage to get out from my hiding place where I felt a little security. Soon, my mom would be looking me over, asking me what I was doing home, and why I hadn't bothered to call. Soon, she would be glaring at me as if to say, "I know what you have been up to and I don't appreciate you coming here and ignoring the elephant in the room." Her eyes could always look into your soul and extract information. It was worse than an interrogation room because I only lied to my mom to make myself feel like I knew something she didn't. Mothers have a sixth sense and they know what we think they don't.

However, my mom stayed in her room. I heard the springing of her bed and her lamp flicked on. She was tucking herself in. "Well that's just great, now I will have to go in there and that makes it ten times more awkward because after I tell her the news, I will just be standing there waiting for a lecture...on the other hand, I could tell her and run out of the room." I thought naively to myself, "Better yet, I am not even going to have a face-to-face conversation. I am already here, she can talk to me if she wants...but I am going to text her." My small purple phone was my saving grace. I began to text.

Hey Mom, I messed up. I have a proble. delete.

Mom, I love you. I am sorr. delete.

Would you forgive me if. delete.

After a few more attempts and failures of typing and deleting what I was going to text her, I felt defeated. Finally, I took one last short breath, gathered my thoughts and sent it. "Mom, please don't be upset. I am sitting on the couch and am really confused about what to do. I am pregnant and I am scared. I tried to do it on my own and I don't know what else to do. I just have a problem and I know that I can fix it. But I really need your help." Listening, I heard my mom's text tone go off, a few shuffles and a sigh, and I began to panic.

By this time, I was drenched in sweat and even more scared to move after the news had been delivered. Slowly, I hear my mom get up and come out into the living room. She looked at me with a calmer look than I would have ever expected. "Is this true?" She inquired, holding up her phone. "Yes." I admitted sheepishly. "What do you mean by this is a problem that you can fix? I don't believe in abortion. There are other options if you are thinking about taking that route." she replied.

I felt a bit more courageous after my mom's calm reaction, so I went on explaining. "Mom, I know that abortion isn't the right thing to do, but many girls have

had it done. I am just confused because I haven't been able to find any information and everyone that I have called has been rude and unfriendly. My questions haven't been answered and I feel like that's the only way to fix the problem. I am not ready for a baby. I can't be like Kayla, that's not the life for me." "There's always adoption. Let's talk about it in the morning. You need to think about it. Try to get some sleep." Unraveling from my blankets that had failed to protect me, I curled up into a ball and after a few hours of watching mind-numbing TV to drown out the looming decisions, I finally drifted off to sleep.

DEBBIE

My daughter told me that she was pregnant in a text. Texted me. Told me. She. Was. PREGNANT. My first thought was that I already knew and should not have been surprised by her text at all. Even if I thought I was prepared, I still found myself with these words echoing in my head. I was disappointed. How could she let this happen? I already had one daughter with two little girls and now another one who wasn't married or ready to take care of a child. She couldn't even take care of herself. Re-reading her text it clicked that she was talking about getting rid of the baby by aborting it...but she had no luck in finding out any information. I do not believe in abortion. I believe that if you get yourself into a situation you should step up and take responsibility for your actions. Did I not instill this in her?

I have tried my best to raise my children with the ability to make right decisions. I knew that the best thing for my daughter was for her not to raise this baby on her own and I was not willing to raise another child at this point in my life. While not wanting to initiate discussing the situation, I got out of bed to go talk to her. No words could describe the stirring in my stomach. I felt like I had failed.

JAMie

The summer was good to me. My friends and I were anticipating infamous vampire movie premieres and time spent by the pool with their babies. Ben and I were about to go to Florida for a friend's wedding where I would be styling all the ladies hair and he would be officiating. In expectation of the vacation/wedding I was also eager to see if I was pregnant. I hoped I was this month as it would give me my ever dreamed of winter baby. Believe me, I planned this. I would take my temperature in the morning and call Ben to come home on his lunch breaks to do the "deed" and make a baby--a baby with his eyes and my smile, his freckles and my curls. We'd pray after, talk about baby names, and how cool it would be the coming Christmas to be hugely pregnant.

I would eventually withdraw money or use my tips from the salon to buy a pregnancy test as Ben loathed me for buying them every month; He preferred I waited until I actually had missed my period before taking the test. Cash left no record of my expenditure. This month, however, I was not pregnant. In my annoyance I buried the once hopeful test in some toilet paper and disposed of the useless, unpromising piece of trash. I was mad again, at everything and everyone; I allowed the emotion to be brief. This month Ben and I were going to take a much needed vacation and I refused to wreck it with my heartbreak. I shut down that part of my brain, that part of my heart, and opened myself to some fun and "suffering for Jesus" in Florida.

During this time, my journal entries reflected hope.

Though I doubted God would be gracious in His giving of a child, I was still amped on Him. I was seeking Him and His words and was incredibly fond of the Message Version of scripture. God was providing for us and we felt set. I was doing the latest workout in hopes of getting in better shape for pregnancy and Florida. Ben and I were doing the best we'd ever been doing, as far as communicating and relating. Though it often seemed very superficial, we were okay with it, because the reality was too much to tackle. We had other activities to engage us including youth ministry, working multiple jobs, and hanging out with our friends.

The occasional "when will you guys start having kids?" or "what have the doctors said is the problem?" would set ablaze something we weren't ready to face. So we casually gave them a staple answer and moved on to asking them questions about their life. All in all, I just felt like I was in a season of want, and want for just one thing. I wanted and yearned for a baby. I wasn't speaking or believing like an heir to Christ. I lacked satisfaction in my womb; the very core of what I believed made me feminine.

Most times, though everything was outwardly good or actually not bad at all, I still felt like I was in a pit. Small things were magnified by my poor attitude and lack of trust that God, my family, and my husband were going to pull through. Because, though my day to day devotions were okay and I ultimately loved God, I honestly didn't trust Him or believe He was for me. This unresolved fact caused me to put misguided trust in others. This was very dangerous, considering humanity is totally imperfect. It only led to a continuing cycle of disappointment.

Devotion We may ask why God chose to put us in the situation we're in. We might call out to Him pleading with Him to explain why we were left behind by a loved one, why our friends abandoned us, why we lost our job, or why someone would want to hurt us. But can we just say that the WHY question isn't what God is going to answer. It's not the question that will change our circumstance, our heart, or our situation.

Let's say a child places his/her hand on the stove and it gets burned. Then they ask their mom, "Why did the stove burn me?" The mother would say, "Because it is hot." But what does this change? The accident still happened. Instead of getting the WHY answer, if we ask how, then the child could have said, "Mom, how can I make the burning go away?" She could then come up with a solution and in the process warn the child not to touch things that are hot in the future and create a learning opportunity that will refine their character. The same is true for us, as His children. If we ask HOW - it allows God to direct our steps and He will guide us to wherever we need to go. If we ask HOW - we are saying to God that we are willing to follow his direction wherever that direction may lead. If we ask HOW - then God will go before us and make a way.

Read Psalm 119:57-72.

Do you believe that God can change your situation? Do you believe He can use this experience for something great?

What does Psalm 119:71 say about suffering?

Do you trust in the path God has set before you? Do

you find it hard to trust Him in all the details?

"The LORD directs the steps of the godly. He delights in every detail of their lives." Psalm 37:23 NLT

"For the word of the LORD holds true, and we can trust everything He does." Psalm 33:4 NLT

When you don't know the direction God wants you to walk, maybe all He wants is for you to be willing to go any direction He needs. We often want to know the will of God for our lives, thinking God wants to keep it a secret. From studying scripture God often wants us to remember His ways and when we find ourselves living the ways of God - we will find ourselves in the will of God.

Our God is a creative God. He created this entire universe. Everything has its purpose. You have never heard a tree ask why it was planted where it was. But God had a plan for that tree; birds live in it, shelter is provided from it, and someone may eventually get some shade from it. If God has a purpose for a tree, don't you think He has a much larger purpose for you? Turn to and trust in God when the big choices arrive and give Him your open heart so that He can do miracles in and through you for the duration of your circumstance. Remain in the ways of God and you most definitely find yourself in the will of God.

"Righteousness will go before him and make his footsteps a way." Psalm 85:13 ESV

JULY

2

"For there is a time and a way for everything, although man's trouble lies heavy on him. For he does not know what is to be, for who can tell him how it will be?"

ecclesiastes 8:6-7

As the days passed, I tried to make a conscious effort to stay at my mom's house. My figure began to subtly change with the progression of the pregnancy, I missed the presence of a man and the comfort I found in the home of Chase, even in the midst of all of our fighting. I began to justify our relationship to myself, as I fought the thoughts of seeking him out. I knew however, that I wouldn't be able to fight them away for long; my mom would not be able to satisfy the discomfort.

My mom walked into the living room and sat down on the couch next to me. She had just gotten home from teaching children with special needs at a local elementary school. I knew that she was a hard worker; she always seemed exhausted at the end of the day. Normally, she would come home and help my little brother with his homework and grade the seemingly never-ending paperwork. However, today, her mind was set on the pursuit to help me.

"Did you want to go to Planned Parenthood and talk to them about your options?" she asked. I studied her face as if looking for a solution, not another appointment. "I have already been there and called them too. They didn't help me. Actually, they were kind of rude and that's why I came here for help. I thought you might have a better idea since you already went through this with Kayla." I answered with a little more snap in my voice than intended. "Well, we can try again if you feel like that's something we should do," Mom half-heartedly whispered as she went for her keys.

The car ride was 20 minutes of silence. I played with my phone while resenting her for making me go somewhere I had already gone. I knew I was right and the fact that this was a dead end frustrated me. Didn't she believe that I had already unsuccessfully explored this option? If I would have succeeded in getting information; I wouldn't have gone home.

As I peered in her direction with a glare on my face, she looked back at me puzzled and questioned the look I was giving her. "What Lesa, why are you looking at me like that?" Mom interrogated me. She was an expert at picking my brain. I didn't like it. "Nothing," I stated defensively. While this one simple word slid out through my teeth, I gritted to contain all my thoughts from exploding in a word bomb. I held back, but it was noticeable. I can't exactly recall how the conversation went from there. I do remember though, that I ended up making my mom extremely mad by my repeated defensive and impolite remarks that I thought proved my point; I was right and we weren't going to get help, especially after we left Planned Parenthood with nothing more than we started with. I thought I had won some sort of battle. In actuality, I had bit the only hand that fed me.

DeBBie

When I initially found out that my daughter had been conspiring about "getting rid" of her baby, I began to call around. People were very rude and didn't even want to talk to me. All I told them was that abortion was something she was thinking about and that I was just looking for information; anything that they thought we should know anything that could help me speak to my daughter. It wasn't just her being informed; I wanted to know how to help her.

Now I could image how frustrated she was when the last person I spoke with just blatantly hung up. I began to wonder where girls turned when they wanted to get information and help. Why was this not readily available to people who needed it? No wonder so many young girls got abortions and procedures they knew nothing about, procedures that would affect them for the rest of their life. Where was the knowledge in the decisions? I told Lesa I would take her to Planned Parenthood, maybe there would be more information that she just had over-looked.

When we got there and went inside and they told us that they could not help us. The only thing they could offer was a pregnancy test and if we wanted anything more we would have to go to the Planned Parenthood in either St. Louis or Kansas City. I was extremely frustrated by this. My daughter looked at me as if begging me to change the outcome of what the lady behind the front desk just told us. I shook my head angrily at the woman. Then turned and shook it sympathetically at my daughter. At this point, I felt just as helpless as she did.

We got back in the car and I was far from happy. I told Lesa she should have found out more before having me drive all the way down there. Defensively she yelled at me and told me that I didn't understand. My skin started to boil. I wanted to pull the car over and tell her to get out. What an ungrateful little girl. I have been searching and searching and this is the kind of attitude I receive? What did she mean by I didn't understand? I understood. I was just as upset as she was. We were now in this together. At least, that's what I thought.

As I lay in bed that night, I thought about my daughter's situation and knew we needed help, but wasn't really sure who to turn to. I knew I could not help her on my own. I had tried, but she just kept arguing with me.

When I woke up the next morning, a name popped into my head: Tina. I knew this was no coincidence. I knew she wanted more children and could maybe meet with Lesa to discuss the possibility of adopting her baby. If nothing else, I would at least have someone to talk to that certainly would pray for Lesa.

I called Tina later that afternoon and explained the situation my daughter was in. She told me that she would begin praying for me and my daughter immediately and meet with Lesa. She was very eager to meet her. I was looking for something to change. Both my daughter and I needed some encouragement and strength. I was in the pursuit of hope.

Resa

After long weeks of no real change, my heart had broken. I thought my mom would be more helpful and I believed she wasn't putting in the effort needed to fix my situation. Why was nobody capable to help me the way I needed; did people just not care enough? She was my own mother; she should have been more outgoing and pushed harder to find where I needed to go. Outraged and confused, I again called my sister.

Fortunately, I called her at the right time. She was only half an hour away, on a mini-vacation with her boyfriend. I could go up for a night and see her. I had stashed away a small tube of meth in my CD player that I could bring and partake in. After all, it had been a few weeks since I last snorted or smoked anything and I could feel the craving. I gathered up the goods and rushed off without even saying good-bye to my mom. I needed to just disappear to get my head straight.

On the way, I received a call from my mom. Not wanting it to be a fight, I tried to keep the conversation quick by giving abrupt, bored replies, until she asked, "Would you want to meet a friend of mine? Her name is Tina and I truly believe she will be able to help you." I rushed to get off the phone as I approached my destination. "Yeah, sounds great. Set it up, text me and let me know when and where she wants to meet." I quickly agreed, then added, "Talk to you later.

My sister stood outside the hotel, smoking a cigarette. She politely guided me where to park. She followed behind me and met me at the edge of the parking lot. Helping me out of the car as if I were an old, fragile woman, she blew out a puff of smoke and

we began chatting. Arm in arm we walked, joked, and laughed our way back to the towering hotel that hid behind a dense wall of trees I loved coming to forget the world and forget the world, I would.

KAYLA

That weekend Charles and I had decided to get a gram of ice (meth) and take a short vacation. We thought it would be relaxing, without kids or responsibilities. We could just get high and do whatever we wanted. We got to the hotel and checked in. It was great! We had sleep number beds, which I had wanted to try for a while!

The first thing we did after unpacking was load a bubble, a small pipe we used to smoke the ice. There were two chairs in the room and we set up the small table as a little 'station'. I then brought out the little baggie of ice. We started to smoke it.

My boyfriend never could light it himself and I hated wasting it so I didn't mind helping every time. After about an hour my thumb was getting a burn callus from the lighter and Charles had begun looking through the small hole in the door for people passing by our room. I hated how paranoid he became after smoking! I tried to tell him to just sit down.

"Babe if we weren't getting high would you be worried about someone coming to our room?" I asked him. I tried to appeal to the logical side of things. "I hear people," he replied still looking out the hole. "We are by the elevator," I pointed out. "No one is going to randomly check on us." I decided we needed to go do something. I put all our stuff away neatly and we got ready to go play laser tag.

On our way to the hotel, my sister called and I invited her up. I didn't really want her to come at first because I wanted to spend some quality time with Charles, and I didn't want her around the drugs since she was pregnant. She met us at the hotel and we drove down the road to play laser tag and glow in the dark miniature golf. I was so high; I wanted to run around because I had so much energy. We played a game of laser tag that Charles won.

Lesa seemed to be in a good mood but I hated how pretty she looked. I had always been a jealous of the attention she got and what I didn't seem to have. I felt like Charles was attracted to her. We then played a round of mini golf. Every room was a different theme and hooked onto the ceiling was a string of black lights. It was dark inside and every object glowed brightly-- even some of the walls. We felt like the game went too quickly so we asked the attendant if we could run back through and take some pictures. He said yes. We spent 2 hours taking a bunch of pictures in every room.

After that we headed back to the hotel. I was wearing down by then and needed some food and a boost. I loaded a bowl for Charles and me and my sister went to get some tacos to bring back. She had some tattoo flyers in her car which we threw out to the people in the parking lot. We laughed and continued with our great time. Settled back in the room after eating, I was ready to get high again. "Do you mind?" I asked my sister. "No, not at all." She responded with a grin, so I lit up. We talked about everything under the sun. I was getting tired and wanted to save some for the next day since we had been using the whole time we had been at the hotel. We needed sleep; we had been up 24 hours prior! Charles didn't want to stop. As much as I didn't want to admit it I knew he was getting addicted.

We loaded bowl after bowl. I made myself stay

awake, not because I wanted to keep getting high, but because I was worried he and my sister would do something together. It was a terrible feeling and I was too scared to say anything to either one about it. So I convinced myself I was just being paranoid and stopped thinking about it. I was so high and tired I started to pass out while hitting the bubble. If anyone knows about meth once you're so high and your body so tired, your mind just starts to shut off and there's nothing you can do. You become delirious, which is the point I was at. So despite all my feelings about Charles and my sister I went to sleep.

When I woke up hours had passed. Charles was still up sitting in the bed. My sister was gone. "Where did she go?" I asked. "She said she had to go home." he replied. I decided to call her just to make sure she was ok. She answered and said she had a great time and that she could get me more drugs when I came through town if I needed it. I hung up the phone, laid down, and gave my aching body the sleep it still longed for. When I woke again Charles was asleep. I woke him up. It was time for us to check out. When I had first fallen asleep we had about a quarter size amount, maybe a little less, of meth left. When I started gathering things up, it was all gone.

I was irritated, not about the drugs but because I would have waited for him, and if I hadn't he would have been very angry with me. He said he was sorry and he accidentally burned it up while I was sleeping, and that my sister assured him she would get us more. So I let it go and we made the journey home. Little did I know he had allowed my sister to finish off the bubble.

lesa

My mom had set me up to meet Tina for lunch at a quiet, locally owned Mexican restaurant a block down the street from her house. I had been dabbling in speed over the weekend and I truly hoped that this woman wouldn't know. I looked scrawny and restless. Being pregnant alone took a lot out of me without the added activities I was partaking in. I took a shower and then made my way down the street. I felt a bit anxious and wondered why I was even meeting with this woman. What other choice did I have though? No one else could provide me with what I needed.

The smell of fajitas and lemons hit my nostrils as I entered into the front door. I wasn't hungry, but I knew I was going to have to force myself to eat to look normal. Plus, the baby was probably hungry. I saw an athletic woman with dark blonde hair waving in my direction. I turned around to make sure she was the woman I was supposed to meet, I didn't see anyone else she could have been waving at; I slowly walked over to the table.

She got up and gave me a hug. She had ordered me water with a lemon in it, perfect; I was craving lemons. I reached for it first thing and put it in my mouth without a second thought. "Have you been craving those?" Tina happily questioned. "Not that I know of, but I do now." I replied.

Tina was extremely polite. She told me about her family while asking me about mine. I had assumed that my mom had already told her most of the things she needed to know, but she entertained the idea of hearing things from my perspective. She leaned in and made eye contact while she listened and waited patiently to talk. I wasn't very good at asking questions, but I tried to be interested in who she was. I didn't really know what to think.

The lunch wrapped up pretty quickly. She spoke a few more encouraging words, gave me a few more hugs and smiled a few more genuine smiles. Her outgoing confidence shined to every dark corner in the restaurant. It was a bit overwhelming at first, but as we finished our meeting, I was drawn to what made her so unique.

With one last hug Tina whispered in my ear, "I will continue to pray for you." I smiled politely back and thought to myself, "Sure, whatever that means." Little did I know the power of those seven words.

Debbie

After seeking for about two weeks, I finally managed to locate a place that could help my daughter and me. A local pregnancy facility, which I heard about from a friend, welcomed us to come and see how far along Lesa was. Lesa didn't seem as interested as I had expected her to be, but I made the final call. We were going. We walked into the lobby and the ladies behind the desk greeted us with warm smiles. I signed my daughter in and we waited. I was thrilled because they said they would do an ultra sound for her. This would be her first ultrasound and we would be able to see how far along she was.

It didn't take long for them to call us back and we got started right away. Lesa appeared to be nervous. I knew that she was confused about whom the possible father was and knowing the exact time of date that the baby was conceived, would yield the truth. I watched as she took a few deep breaths as the gel was applied to her stomach and then turned to look at the screen. We both gasped at the little baby, no bigger than a grape. My daughter smiled, bringing tears to my eyes. We finished with recording the pace of the baby's heartbeat. The baby was strong, healthy, and growing quickly.

At this point, they couldn't give an exact date, but the technician estimated she had been pregnant for around twelve weeks. She then cleaned Lesa up and asked if we would like to speak with a mentor, someone that could give us more information on the options. Quickly, both my daughter and I shook our heads YES.

The mentor empathized with Lesa and took the time to inform her about her options: abortion, mothering, and adoption. As we continued talking, Lesa made it clear that abortion was no longer an option, especially after seeing her baby for the first time in the ultrasound. I believed that the ultrasound saved this baby's life. Expressing her doubts, she inquired about adoption, asking, "What if the family doesn't love him? What if I never get to see him? What if he has side effects from the drugs I have been doing? The mentor reassured us "nothing was certain."

lesa

A few days later and my mom and I were quarreling again. Why was there no peace? Tired and annoyed, it seemed to be one thing after another. I was always in a fight with someone. There was no rest for me and I was extremely irritated because I hadn't had even a small dose of my Desire. The mood swings and cravings to get high had built a brick wall between me and my mom and I was on edge. I felt like all she was trying to do was tear me down and I was tired of trying to rebuild myself back up. So I just lost it. I angrily cursed and yelled at her until we were both trying to yell over each other. Then I said it; I said the final breaking curse word, but my mom ended the fight.

"That's it. I have had enough," my mom screamed back at me through tears, "Get OUT!!" "Fine, I will. If that's what you want. I hope I die." I shouted as I ran into my room, flustered by hearing the same two words again from someone I loved. I grabbed a few items of clothing and rapidly shoved them into a plastic bag.

As I heard my mom's sobs from the front room, I put my head down, walked right past her, out the door, and slammed it behind me. Thick sheets of icy water poured from the heavens; small pellets of hail began to hit me as I made my escape. Even the sky was dark and dismal. I was glad that I wasn't the only thing in the universe that felt all messed up.

Immediately, I cranked my wind shield wipers up to top notch. The rain that sloshed over the glass had become like a blanket, covering the only place I could see out of. I turned on my radio just in time to hear flash flood warnings blaring. Great I thought, of all the nights to be thrown out! I wasn't sure where I was going; I just knew I couldn't get very far in the flash flood weather that was occurring all around me. Roads were closing and the clock was ticking. I decided I would try contacting Tina. Maybe I could stay at her place. I called her crying and she confirmed that it was absolutely okay for me to stay the night with her. She said she would get a place ready for me in the basement and that I would have my own little room. It sounded good. I got directions and about five minutes later, my phone died.

Speedily, I drove a little longer down the road toward Tina's house. The puddles kept getting deeper and deeper; my car ended up completely submerged. I kept my foot on the gas and just prayed that I would make it through. I knew I had told my mom I had wanted to die, but I really wasn't ready. The water began to come in through the cracks in my windshield and the vents in my dashboard. My feet were soaked and my hands were sweating. I gripped the steering wheel, the radio turned off and for a split second I began thinking that this was it.

Then out of nowhere, my car made it through the risen water and the road that had been flooded was now being closed off. Cars were being told to reroute. Policemen and firemen were closing off both sides of the street that I had just gone through and, by some kind of miracle, made it out of. I looked into my rear view mirror to see that three cars behind me had tried to brave the flood like I did and all had become stranded in the middle of the waters at the merciless hand of the rain.

My radio flicked back on and more warnings were issued, including my location. I was stuck in a donut; on every side of me there was flooding. Hungry and in need of some gas, I stopped at the only gas station in the middle of the storm. Apparently, everyone else had stopped there too. It was packed. I parked at a gas pump and grabbed my hooded sweatshirt from the back seat in an effort to stay as dry as possible.

The gas station attendee greeted me as I entered the store. I was going to need something to help me through until I could get to Tina's. I grabbed a candy bar and an energy drink and made my way back to the front. Before I could get there I ran into someone I knew. "Hey, what are you doing here Sandra?" I was surprised to see her. Sandra was a friend of Chase's. I had resented her when I first met her because I felt like Chase was cheating on me with her. At this point, I didn't care. I knew that she did what I did and I assumed that whoever she was with would probably have a few rocks of meth on him. So, I manipulated the situation and gave her the "pity me" speech.

I told her about how my mom and I had gotten into it and I had no place to go. I said my car didn't seem to want to work in this weather because it had been submerged in the water. She said she was headed into the city. Yes, this is exactly what I had planned. "What part are you going to; may I ride along with you?" I asked hopeful. "Sure, that's fine with me," Sandra shrugged and stood by me as I quickly paid and grabbed my stuff. "I need to lock up my car and then I will come with you," I happily announced.

"We will be waiting right here," she said as she climbed into the car with a man I had never seen before.

Secretly extremely pleased at the way this night was turning out. I grabbed my keys, locked up, and left my car in front of the gas pump. I had this gut feeling that I should move it, but if they had drugs, I wasn't going to waste their time. The man looked at me as I climbed into the back.

At first, no one said anything. Due to the inclement weather, we had to take a thirty minute detour in the opposite direction of where I wanted to go. Then Sandra began getting antsy. This was the opportunity I had been waiting for. I watched her fumble around in her purse and pull out a familiar, small glass bubble. I couldn't help but get excited. "Let's pull over and take a break. I don't want to light up and get stopped by a cop. That's the last thing we need," she stated.

We parked in the middle of a subdivision under construction. If anything, I felt like we stuck out like a sore thumb. We sat in the car at a curb, where there was not even one house or car in sight. They passed the pipe back and forth and I had assumed that they were going to pass it to me, but then the man spoke for the first time to me since I had been in the car.

"Sandra told me that you are pregnant and although my wife did this stuff with our boys, I don't want to be liable for your baby having any problems." The stranger held the pipe again and then added, "It's not because I don't want to share. Do you understand?" "Yeah, that's understandable. I wouldn't want you to do anything you didn't feel comfortable with," I said with a smile on my face, although inside I was burning. Who was this guy to tell me what to do? He didn't even know my situation. I don't look pregnant, I thought. I should be able to do what I want. This isn't his life. I realized I had been sitting on the edge of my seat, unbuckled in anticipation, but now in light of this new information I just received, I scooted back into my seat and nestled my head into my hood. "Get me out of this car", I cried in the back of my mind.

It seemed like an eternity before they started driving again. By this point, my phone had been dead for hours. I realized that Tina would be wondering what happened to me because I had abandoned the original plans. I had not let her know that I was no longer coming to her house. Nobody knew where I was. My car was probably still stranded at the gas station and I was like a ghost, off the radar. I liked it that way.

Finally, we made it into the city; I asked Sandra if she could take me to my friends. She didn't have a problem with me getting high, so I invited her to come with. I explained to her that he had an endless amount and would give it to her for free. I enjoyed hanging out with him and knew that she would enjoy his company too. I didn't want her to meet him; I was jealous for his attention. However, this was the only way I could get what I wanted.

At last, at around three in the morning, we made it to Stephen's house. I had plugged my phone in at Sandra's to let him know to be expecting us. When we got there, he opened up the door, eager to see me. I loved the charismatic way he made a girl feel welcome. "Hello Desire, goodbye World," I speculated under my breath as I took one last look out into the rainy world just beyond the door that was closing with no regrets.

JAMIE

I searched for words to make sense of what had just happened, I found myself grabbing my wallet and keys on my venture out of my house. To ensure my point was getting across, I slammed the front door with all the strength I had. I wanted to walk away from a man that didn't deserve the disaster I always seemed to bring him. I couldn't handle another month of disappointment, for his sake as much as mine.

The wind of another negative pregnancy test blew on angry emotional cinders, igniting a fight over his failure to take out the trash as he had promised. The frustration of deceiving cycles and financial insecurities blew on the small flame of a broken promise - creating an inferno of hurt and anger. Crude words had escalated into throwing things, then to slamming everything in sight and swinging only to miss my husband. When the laptop shattered and Ben had my arms restrained, my emotions met with reality; I had to leave. I was ashamed. God seemed nowhere in any corner of that room, or in the house for that matter. My husband bewildered sat on his knees silent on the floor, trying to reassemble our valuable marriage.

I had no direction, extremely strong convictions and resounding condemnation. I drove for hours. My drive resembled my life: hopeless, misguided, angry and reckless. I embraced what the enemy was saying and kept driving. The sun was shining and the sky was incredible. It was the early part of the day. How could I ruin such an incredible day with the person I loved most? Did I truly love him; how in the world did love look like that? Now I had all day to think about what I had done.

I stopped to text my closest friend to tell her I was walking away from my marriage. My husband deserves a life-giving, baby-carrying, nurturing bride. This was such a displaced text for her - considering all she knew is we had trouble conceiving and teased heavily about being annoyed with one another. She knew there was really nothing to say - but that she would be there for us both by praying intentionally.

I ignored calls from Ben for hours as I wrestled with a barrage of questions. Where am I going to live? What will our friends say? What will the church say? Why did God hate me so much? I felt even more hopeless knowing if I continued this way I was going to lose my whole life of friends, relationships, and security. In this season of bitterness I believed it would be easy for those outside our walls, including my parents, to blame me; this only made me feel more defeated.

The sad part was this wasn't the first time, yet it was very much the worst time. I can't go back. I can't keep doing this. I can't handle the next time being even worse than this. As I look back on this season of my life I was obviously buying what the enemy was selling. I wasn't in a mature emotional or spiritual state. The 'me now' would tell the 'me then' to start speaking the truth of God's Word and transform the way I was thinking.

As much as I'd think the 'old me' would heed the 'new me's' advice - I also know that my 'old me's' heart ached with the reality that I was unable to conceive and I was unable to have a life- giving marriage if I didn't. That was my truth – my reality, no matter how misplaced. I had to journey through this wilderness to get to the Promised Land. The journey of emotional and spiritual maturity is a testament of God's goodness and a whole other story. As much as it hurt my image and pride to admit, it was where I was at.

The lies I bought from the enemy were numerous. I believed I was inadequate, flawed, damaged beyond repair, a joke, and a pathetic excuse of a woman. I thought I was being punished for not being pure when I first became a believer. I believed I deserved being infertile from all the times I pleaded with God to not let me become pregnant in high school and college. I thought I wasn't a woman but rather a little girl stuck in a young woman's body.

I believed God didn't trust me to raise a human being. I thought my recent behavior certainly supported that lie. In desperation, I cried so hard my head hurt. I pulled into a local park and slipped into the back seat to nap.. Kids screamed in joy while they played outside.

To my despair, the world continued on as I wished mine would end. I had failed, in a big way. I was ashamed at how much ugliness was still in my heart. Again, the enemy assaulted me with questions. Am I even saved? Does God continue to move and think of me when I behave this way? My disrespect seemed to add an even deeper sense of failure on my long list of shortcomings. I was useless and unnecessary. My husband could do, and deserved, better.

In my tide of tears and swollen eyes I drifted to sleep. My last utterance was a plea to not wake up. I asked for forgiveness, in case the good Lord agreed and took me away. I woke up sweating, to a car door shutting next to mine. I had only been asleep for less than an hour. I'm awake. Jesus didn't take me. This is dumb. It was time to go home, where I could eat and decide my next move.

Surely Ben was done with this. How could a man endure so much unnecessary drama? I remained in my car for a long moment. This is it; he is done too, I know it. I walked in to find my husband waiting for me, Bible opened next to him and in the middle of journaling. Upon shutting the door behind me more humbly than when I left, my groom embraced me. The atmosphere was different. He looked into my eyes, and with all seriousness, proclaimed, "God isn't done with us yet. I'm willing to adamantly pursue adoption. God has assured me nothing is impossible or out of reach for Him to accomplish." For the first time in what seemed like months my husband was standing in the gap for our marriage, for me, for our dream of being parents.

Until this moment, he had been pretty reluctant to see adoption as an alternative for starting a family. It was more of a distant idea and only an option after we had biological children. For the first time since our wedding he was seeing me. In his grace, I saw the grace of my Heavenly Father. Ben was waiting for me, open to anything but only if it was with me. He made me feel necessary, desired, and worth fighting for. We scheduled to attend an introduction class held in a few weeks by one of the two agencies we were interested in. We went from hopeless to hopeful. Adoption felt right, made us feel spiritually full and captivated us more than we thought it ever would.

Devotion

God doesn't promise that we won't go through rough water. He doesn't promise that we won't get stuck in hard places. He doesn't promise that hard times won't come our way. However, He does promise that when we feel stuck and alone, it's not a dead end. Although we may not feel Him, He is with us through thick and thin, and He promises us that He will get us back. It may not be as fast as we think it should, but be patient. God's rescue always comes in perfect timing.

He is a personal God, who wants nothing but the best for us, but that doesn't mean the best would be to take us out of the situation we are in. Nothing we experience shocks God. Everything we endure and walk through has been sifted through the hands of the Almighty. Sometimes, it doesn't make sense that God would allow us to walk through bankruptcy, or have a family member or friend pass away, nor does it make sense that we become homeless, victims of abuse, or deeply wounded by close friends.

God is a God of choice. We all make choices and we do to that can drastically affect others (positively and negatively). God allows, but He never orchestrates, sin. He allows humanity to choose right living or destruction. Being victims of our own or other's sin never makes sense and seems so unjust. However, God permits it. God always cares more about our heart and character more than our comfort. He wants to see our hearts change before our situation does. And He is always able to work out EVERYTHING "for the good

of those who love God and are called according to his purposes." (Romans 8:28NLT)

Why do you think God has allowed the circumstances that surround you?
Check out Hebrews 2:16-18.
Read Verse 18 again. What is the Promise God makes to us?

In God's grace, He sent Jesus. Jesus was created to understand the trials we face on a daily basis; When He died on the cross for us and sent the Holy Spirit to be our guide, He would know exactly how to lead us because He already faced EVERYTHING we are now up against. Whether our problems are big or small, they are all important to Him. Give Him your burdens and be willing to give Him your heart so that He may provide the escape route that you have been longing for.

"Don't be afraid, I've redeemed you. I've called your name. You're mine. When you're in over your head, I'll be there with you. When you're in rough waters, you will not go down. When you're between a rock and a hard place, it won't be a dead end--Because I am GOD, your personal GOD, The Holy of Israel, your Savior. That's how much you mean to me. That's how much I love you. I'd sell off the whole world to get you back, trade the creation just for you." Isaiah 43:2-4 MSG

august

3

"If only I knew where to find God; I would go to His court. I go east, but He is not there. I go west, but I cannot find Him. I look to the south but He is concealed. "But He knows where I am going. And when He tests me, I will come out as pure as gold."

JOB 23:3, 8-10

Lesa

Sketch pad in hand and a bunch of colorful markers, I found myself transfixed in a drawing frenzy for hours. It turned out that Stephen's daughter was staying the weekend with him and it was extremely inconvenient for me as she kept coming into his room to use the markers I was so attached to. I thought to myself, "doesn't she have a movie to watch?"

Annoyed, I yanked Stephen aside to talk to him. Before I could even get one word out of my mouth, the jealous little girl who hated that I stole her daddy's attention, squirmed between us. I gave Stephen a glare that said, "If you don't remove this little girl from my sight, I am going to scream." So he took her into the other room and set her up to watch cartoons on her netbook he had given her. It was one that he had tried to fix many times and never the less, still crawled at an unimpressive speed.

I slammed shut his bedroom door as soon as he left and impatiently waited for him to return--hoping it would be without his daughter. I laid back down on the black futon, grabbed the sketch pad, and started tracing the lines over and over with different colors until the paper tore, and the ink bled into the next few pages. It was a mess. Frustrated and anxious, I grabbed my phone to see if anyone had tried to reach me.

A few missed calls from my sister.

A few missed texts from some friends.

A few missed calls from Tina.

I was surprised. I really had no intention of talking to anyone. I was intent on staying right where I was. I picked up the bubble and set my phone back down. Immediately it began to ring. Tina's number flashed onto the screen and I was terrified. What was I going to tell her? I couldn't tell her the truth. There was an urge however, to answer and explain to her why I hadn't come to her house.

I ignored the call and walked out into the living room where Stephen and his daughter sat. His little girl looked up at me and did not hesitate to ask me if I wanted to play--begging me to spin her. My phone began ringing again. "I can't be around you right now!" I yelled down at the little girl. She whimpered and then ran, crying to her daddy. He looked at me and shook his head. "You don't talk like that to little girls," he snapped.

"I am getting a call and I really need her to be quiet. I will be in the garage. Keep her in here. I don't want anyone to know I am here." I snapped back. Quickly, I closed the garage door and answered in one motion; I began the call that I thought I could talk my way out of.

"Hey Tina, Sorry I missed your calls. I was down by the pool and forgot my cell. I really just needed to get away from everyone and clear my head." I repeated what I was saying back to myself to make sure I didn't sound as high as I felt.

"Oh, well I was really disappointed that you didn't come over last night. I was hoping we could talk. I am glad you are with a friend and are trying to calm down. I would like to see you today if that's okay," she hinted back.

The burning of my lies flustered me and I knew she could see right through them. Paranoia set in. "Well, I am not sure the address of where I am, but I am going to be at the pool just hanging out, so if you want to come see me you can. I don't know how long I will be here. We are just two girls, soaking up some sun." I said with the assumption that it was what she wanted to hear. I then waited for her to say her good-byes but to my horror, she replied, "well, I am in the city, so ask your friend where you are and I will meet with you." Stuck in my lie, I couldn't go back now. "Sure. Give me one second. I have to go down to the pool and ask her. I will call you back," I lied. I hung up and ran into the other room where Stephen was now half-awake and his daughter was running amuck.

"Hey, can you take me to Sandra's. I have a friend that wants to check up on me and I really need to get over there. I don't want her to know I am here and I have to look like I am doing okay. Can you please take me?" I begged.

"Hun, anyone who sees you is going to know you're high. Plus, she doesn't have a pool and you don't have a bathing suit. I guess I can take you if you need me too," He offered with a displeased look on his face.

"Thank you," I replied.

I called Tina back and let her know that I would be in Sandy's apartment, but to call me when she got there and I would come down. I told her the general location, but not the exact apartment number in case anything went rogue. She said she would be there in fifteen. I dampened my hair in the sink to make it appear as if I had been swimming, then I threw one of Stephen's T-shirts onto my bony body along with some shorts. I slid into some flip flops and we jumped into his car to head to Sandy' to keep my lie from failing.

As he turned the key, the motor made a putting sound and then died. "No, this can't be happening!" I thought, "I have to get to Sandra's or I will be caught." I looked at Stephen in sheer fright and begged him to get the car running. Fifteen minutes had gone by and another phone call from Tina seemed to taunt me. Just as I pressed ignore, my stomach sank. I knew that we wouldn't be able to get to Sandra's on time, I turned off my phone. I went back inside with Stephen and tried to pretend like it wasn't a big deal, but the sweat on my forehead told him otherwise. He began his guessing games as soon as we walked back into the house. I wasn't sure what to tell him, so I lied again.

"It was nobody, just an old friend that I wanted to see because I haven't seen them in a while." The lies just kept coming out, I couldn't stop them.

He studied me for a minute and then quit asking after realizing he wasn't going to get another word out of me. I couldn't keep my lies straight and he knew that. So, instead of interrogating me further, he invited me to come relax in his room and cool down from whatever it was that I was dealing with. His daughter asleep on the couch was a nice break and I was more than ready for another hit of the pipe.

I turned my phone back on to text Sandra and see what she was doing, I realized I had about five missed calls. My heart sank. I don't know why I felt like I had to justify my actions to her. Why was she being so persistent? As I tried hard to block it out, my brain was going faster than I. Unaware of how long it had been both Stephen and I turned our eyes to the security camera monitors that presented a suspicious SUV sitting right outside his door. I knew exactly who it was and I was baffled as to how Tina found me.

After my odd behavior and seemingly endless ringing phone, paranoia told Stephen's mind that something was not right. "Who is that?" Stephen questioned me with no room for error. "That's one of my mom's friends, she won't leave me alone. Let's just stay in here and wait until she goes away." I suggested, watching my phone ring over and over. He looked at me with blame in his eyes. Stephen's paranoid accusations grew. "Is that a cop; are you a cop?!?! I think you better leave before there's trouble," he yelled.

Not wanting this to escalate further, I fearfully opened the door and walked outside with the intention of getting rid of the woman who was ruining my high and causing havoc. With the thought that I would talk my way out of this again, I assumed I would be right back in and when she was gone, Stephen would calm down. I couldn't be any more wrong.

"Hey Lesa, what are you doing here? I think you need to come with me. Everyone is worried about you." She looked at me eagerly. "We just got over here and my phone died. Sorry I didn't call to tell you where I was. Everything is fine though," I replied. I knew she saw through my lie. I could feel my already dilated pupils expanding. "You need to come with me. Get in," she pleaded. Tina began to look more concerned and the underlying tone of trouble was a foot. I could tell; it was time for me to go. Sadly, I took one last look at the townhouse toward the security cameras, I conceded defeat and climbed into the car. As we drove further and further away, I realized that this was the first time in days, that I had seen the sun face to face.

Kayla

I was hanging out at my mom's house doing some laundry, when my phone rang. Tina was calling.

"Hello." I said. "How are you doing today?"

She didn't waste any time. "Do you know where your sister might be?"

I thought for a moment. "No, I am not sure where she is. Is something wrong?"

"I think she is doing drugs again. Do you know where she goes?"

I thought about answering for a minute. If I told her, I would be giving up my sister, but the safety of her baby overwhelmed my loyalty and I answered. "If she's doing drugs, I know where she is." I proceeded to give Tina the exact directions to Lesa's drug dealer's house.

I told her to park in the first parking lot before she got to his house and to walk through the stairwell to the other side of the building so she wouldn't be seen on the security cameras. I had also been there to get high and I knew the layout. Her dealer was so paranoid he had two cameras on at all times and constantly sat in his room watching them. I had lost more hours than I would like to admit staring into the very same TV screen, watching for cars I knew to drive by, watching for the police to pull up, watching for anything.

I hoped my sister wasn't there and that Tina would call me to tell me she was wrong, I tried to call her myself, but she didn't answer. I tried to text Stephen, no answer there either. "God, please keep her and her baby safe." I prayed as I waited.

Lesa

Shame, anger, bitterness and embarrassment filled me up as quick as air can fill a balloon. What should have been a fifteen minute car ride felt like an eternity. I could feel my face burning, my head spinning, and my nerves shaking. With my eyes glued to the ground, I began cursing at my situation. Unaware that I might be saying anything aloud, Tina started talking firmly to me. I was unsure how to react to her. I preferred yelling, because then I could yell back. This was much worse.

"Do you understand what you are doing? You are killing your baby. Do you care about yourself? Do you care about anyone?" Tina inquired and kept at it with a penetrating tone, "What's your ten year goal? Do you even know what you are going to be doing then? Will you still be doing this? Will you even be here if you keep going down this road? How about five years? We are going to get you a drug test..."

My ears pounded and her words blurred together. My mind began to repeat the words that cut at my heart, slashing deep wounds that left me gasping. "Killing. Do you Care? Ten years. Where are you? Five Years? Drug test."

Frantically, I tried to answer her questions, I couldn't. I didn't know where I would be. I had never given any thought about the future. This shamed me and my eyes started pouring, mascara running down my face. Then it sunk in. I was killing myself. I was killing this baby. I was destined for destruction if I kept walking the same way. Depression reared its ugly head and then anger took its place. Why was she getting me a drug test? She already knew I was high. We didn't need a test to confirm that. Only five minutes until home and even that future scared me. Why would I want to think of five years? I was about to seal my fate.

Once at Tina's house, she sent me first thing to the bathroom to take the test that I already knew would yield positive results. Although, I believed it was the biggest waste of time, I complied and took the test. Afterward, I felt even worse. I could no longer deny my reality. I could no longer pretend like everything was okay; it wasn't.

Downstairs there was a room set up for me as she had anticipated my arrival the night before. Tina handed me a few clean blankets to snuggle up in. "The basement stays colder than the rest of the house." She explained. She then tucked me in and said her goodnights. As soon as she left, she unknowingly abandoned me in a battle with an enemy she could not see--my inevitable thoughts.

JAMIE

I have always found it interesting how much human nature clings to hope--the chance for something new. It's in the newness of the season that we find ourselves doing things differently, seeing the Word in a new way and stirred back to life--as if the season before was but a distant memory. After the hopeful feeling wore off, daunted became Ben and I's feeling of choice. Still immature in our faith and unaware of how to align our thoughts with His truth, my husband and I began to believe our new and hopeful endeavor was now a lost cause.

In our times with the Lord we would feel strengthened and jointly believe He had called us to adopt. It seemed, though, as soon as we researched agencies, started paperwork, and saw the initial bottom dollar, that renewed "soar on the wings of eagles" feeling of strength and expectation vanished. The stress created a deepened sense of inadequacy and even made us question our thinking. Why weren't we seeing anything clearly? We decided our only measure to advance this call was to pray; the rest was in God's hands. Nightly, my husband would say the same prayer regarding our receiving a baby. It was different than before, when we wanted to naturally have a baby--it was a big plea, every night. It would sound much like this:

"Lord, you know all things. We believe you want to give us a child, a healthy baby through adoption. Lord, pay for all of it, supply all our needs to take care of them and perform on our behalf. You know the truest desires of our hearts. Amen."

Most nights, it was all we prayed about. We would thank God in heaven for providing all of our needs and then pray for our baby. Other nights we would blend the needs of others in it--but it was always in our prayers. As I look back, Ben and I became edified and even chuckled about how 'immeasurably more' He provided.

One evening, I was asked to host a sale booth full of items that I had hand crafted to help fund our adoption. I had recently returned from Haiti and was even more stirred to get my hands on a baby. I was unaware that the event was an 'Adoption Awareness Event'; God is uncanny like that.

At this time, Ben was still a little apprehensive and preferred I got pregnant rather than face the grueling task of paper work and the unknown. What began as an evening of helping me turned into checking out other tables. As he came back to my booth--from roaming, a spark accompanied him. He marveled at all that was available-- all the things we had been searching for, for weeks--a glimmer of hope had been injected in him and it was obvious.

The evening closed and we broke down our tables. We began to walk around and look at what was still left. We visited some booths and got some pamphlets and enjoyed some small talk. We rounded a corner and were instantly captivated by a small booth in the back. The table was sponsored by a local church with a ministry that resourced several adoption agencies--the church members had personal experience with. The table was run by a couple who had, themselves, adopted--finally, someone on the same page! The connection was instant to the husband and wife who had a story with a hopeful ending. We talked for what seemed like minutes--in reality it had been an hour--unfazed by the booths tearing down around us. We ended our conversation in tears, a prayer, and hugs.

On our way out, Ben and I were stopped by the event coordinator who had noticed our conversation and wanted details. We caught up for a minute and then continued out. As we braced ourselves for the cold weather that made its abrupt appearance--we were stopped again. The husband that had talked, cried, and prayed for us--with more focus on Ben than I--handed Ben a book. When "Adopted for life" by Russell Moore was placed into his hands, there was a spiritual exchange. As if for the first time, a man was affirming Ben to press forward--that this was indeed his calling and that it was okay to embrace it and fall in deep.

It's much different for a man than a woman. Naturally, a man desires to conquer a woman, spread his seed and multiply. A woman can nurture anything in sight. Young girls can play baby dolls, brush each other's hair and pretend tea and kitchen all day long. Men are more literal. Give me this--I make that--there it's made. Women, we nurture it. My intention isn't to make men sound like mindless, He-men, but rather to point out that they are literal, factual, conquering, feeling the responsibility to produce, direct, solution makers. To embrace adoption, the 'out of the box' alternative to being a family--is harder for a man than a woman because they play no part in making a solution or producing a result. They are just as necessary as the woman but don't feel necessary at all. This simple 'rite of passage' act--infused Ben on a new level that ultimately became unstoppable. It's amazing the influence men have on each other.

From that moment on--things seemed to fall into place. I met a woman who had a successful; adoption through an organization we'd admired and felt strongly drawn to. The structure, fundamentals, wisdom, and years of experiences drew us to our agency. From there we attended an introduction event to inform prospective families. Everything about it captivated us. We began the paperwork and waited for God to provide the means. We were once again hopeful. This was it. Our paperwork reflected our interest in international adoption from Haiti and Guatemala. We were making progress.

Devotion

We were designed to be emotional beings--to feel the power of being in love and the peace of trusting the Almighty. However, after the Fall of Man - through the disobedience of Eve then Adam - our feelings have been manipulated and used to draw us away from the true intentions of the Father. Anger, bitterness, hurt, and jealously are all emotions we weren't created for. Because of that, the energy that is expended trying to maintain all these emotions gets very heavy. These emotions buzz at us like mosquitos and like mosquitos they suck the life out of us a little at a time. They don't want to leave because they know that we will provide what they need. If we continue to live in these unintended emotions they eventually overwhelm us, change us, and even define us. When in full bloom they produce a life that in itself is very lifeless. All hope seems lost and we live every single day lost, unproductive and unrestored.

But what if we told you there was rest--the kind that can be found even when you're battling. It's the rest that can be felt even when you have worked hard all week to earn that dollar, to fight away harsh thoughts, or struggled with the fight to get out of bed each day. It's the rest that God prepared for you and all He asks in return is the love and devotion of your heart and intentions.

Be encouraged to Read Hebrews 4:9-11(a).
What does it say about God's rest?
What is it that you need rest from? Do you believe

that it's okay to take a day to revitalize in preparation for the battles your facing? Are you making time every day to rest and be still in the Presence of the Almighty?

What does it say God himself did on the last day of creating the world?

God is calling. He is asking for your heart. He doesn't want you to suffer and strive for the things this world can offer. The world can never offer satisfaction, it will never be enough. There is no relationship like the one with Jesus. There is nothing that can be felt like it. God is not about rules and regulations; He wants to be with YOU. He will meet you where you are and He will lead you to where you need to go. When Jesus rescues you, you have complete freedom. You don't want to go back to doing the things you were doing not because of the "rules" but because of the Love. Devotion isn't about going to church on sunday. Only devoting one day to God on sunday is religion. Devoting your daily activities to Him--that's a relationship!

"You did not choose me. I chose you. I appointed you that you should go and bear fruit and that your fruit should abide, so that whatever you ask the Father in my name, he may give it to you." John 15:16 ESV

September

"Say to those with fearful hearts, be strong, do not fear; your God will come, He will come with vengeance; with divine retribution He will come to save you." Isaiah

35:4-5

Resa

I laid in bed and wallowed in self-pity. The darkness in the room paired with the lack of windows created a tomb-like environment. My heart was beating faster than a fluttering hummingbird's wings and I couldn't stop crying. I was too high to sleep, even though that was all I wanted to do. I wanted to go to sleep and never wake up. I was so ashamed of myself; the world overpowered me as I lay there being smothered by my own thoughts. Alone was the scariest place to be.

I held tightly to my stomach and completely broke down. I was at the end of my rope and couldn't live this way any longer. Should I just kill myself? Everyone was upset with me and I wasn't strong enough to have this baby. The baby would just grow up to hate me just as much as I hated myself.

All of the sudden, an unusual feeling emerged. I wiped away the few tears that trickled down my eyes with my palm and wiped my nose on my t-shirt. I blubbered into the darkness, "God, is that you?" Unaware of why I said that, I felt crazy. Without warning, I felt a tugging at my heart to get out of bed and fall onto my knees. I listened intently; My heart slowed down and throbbed loudly. I put my hands together, placed them over my heart to keep it from beating out of my chest, and asked again, "God, is that you?"

Restless, a voice whispered into my ear, "Talk to me, I will understand. I will take this burden you are carrying and I will provide you peace. Let me in; I won't abandon you. Confess to me all you have done and lay your worries and burdens at my feet. Let me take them from you. I love you." Tears burst from my eyes again and prayers sprouted from my lips, flowing like a river; I began to plead before God and spill out all the wrongs I had done. My unclean mouth burned as I released the anger from my heart. I didn't want to hold onto it anymore. I couldn't stand the pain and grief of my selfishness. I was unworthy and undeserving of this acceptance.

Who had I become? I sobbed. The shame was unbearable. "I have been here the whole time," God continued as I hid my face, "I have not abandoned you, I have not forsaken you. I have watched over you and I have loved you. Let me be your rescue. Take my hand and walk with me."

For most of my life I had believed that God never existed, but there on my knees, He made Himself undeniably real. My heart melted into a puddle of acceptance and I let it open up to receive the new life He spoke of, wanting with all my heart to believe it would save me.

I continued to pray and ask in expectancy that God would take care of my baby--that He would let my baby experience the Love that was in the room and that He would never take His hand off of him.

At this moment, I realized that God had put this willing heart in my stomach to break open the hardened one in my chest. The planning and preparation God had put into this moment, was indescribable. Peace fell over me, a surreal calmness I had never before felt. All the weight lifted from my chest and I emerged feeling brand new. The drug high had subsided and the darkness was no longer overpowering. I gathered myself up off the floor, my mind and heart renewed, feeling like an outsider looking in; I knew my life would never be the same.

When the room got quiet, my heart still stirred; I felt an urgency to go tell Tina what had just happened. Excited and scared I walked slowly up the stairs, not wanting to run into her children or husband. I looked terrible as I had not slept all night. The puffiness of my eyes bulged and as I touched my face, I knew that I appeared restless and pathetic. When I found myself about halfway up the stairs, I heard paper rustle.

Nervous, I walked a little further and peeked through the handrail into the living room. There Tina was, sitting with an open book in the quiet of the morning with a cup of coffee. My curiosity got the best of me and I fearfully walked up a few more steps. That's when she saw me.

While I waited for her to say something, she just smiled. Unsure about how to respond back, I stuttered, "Do you have any books I can read?" "Sure, we have a library just right over here." She got up to show me. "You don't have to get up, you're fine. I will look if you don't mind." "Help yourself. If you're hungry for breakfast just let me know. Make yourself at home." Tina compassionately suggested and then went back to her reading.

I made my way across the living room and into the library; I noticed that Tina was reading the Bible. I had seen Bibles before, but not with the markings that this one had. It was cluttered with writing all over the pages. I was swamped by shelves lined up with many books, and was unsure what I should choose. I began to pull out books by their spines and look over them. Books

about drugs, mystery, and heartache caught my attention, but didn't keep it. Two hundred books deep, I stumbled upon 'The Lies That Women Believe'. All the other books shriveled in comparison. My eyes lit up.

A spacious nook summoned me from the corner of their sitting room. A cozy blue chair invited me to sit and read. Jumping right in, the first page boldly confronted me. As I flipped through the book, the lies I had believed about God were numerous. For the first time, I understood who I had spoken to; here at 19 years old, my life had just begun.

Debbie

As hard as it was to discipline the children I love, I know it was the best thing I could have done when I told my daughter to leave. Although the emotions were dramatic, tension was high, and I spoke in anger, when she left my heart broke. I knew it was out of my control.

My daughter returned to me, weeks later with apologies, and though I wasn't sure what to expect this time, forgiveness always had a place in my heart for my kids. I hurt for my girls, but I was moved by each apology and held onto hope that the road ahead would hold less apologies and heartache, and that our relationships would no longer be strained, but strengthened. Graciously, I listened .

I knew there was something different about her. I no longer sensed that I was enabling her to do the wrong things by letting her live with me. Our relationship slowly began to build as she looked to me as someone who could help and be trusted. I worked often; if I am quite honest, probably too often but I knew my daughter needed help.

She would need a doctor and some form of insurance to cover the cost of her pregnancy. Unsure of how the whole process worked, I knew the urgency that Lesa had, even if she didn't. Tina came to my rescue by offering to take Lesa to get her Medicaid, set up her doctor's appointments, and then drive her to and from the places that she needed to be. It was a blessing! Amazed at her generosity, I quickly agreed to the answered prayer that I had yet to pray.

Lesa

I anxiously awaited my first doctor appointment, not knowing what to expect. I was excited and nervous and prayed that my baby was healthy. Tina was going with me to my first one and I was grateful that I wasn't going alone. I disliked talking to people I didn't know, it was far from my comfort zone. I had never been in charge of anything, not even my own life. Tina picked me up and we chatted the entire way to the local health clinic. This woman could talk a mile a minute, always encouraging me and then asking me about the intentions I had. I couldn't always answer fast enough before she would continue rambling on. To be quite honest, I would usually end up with a headache before getting to the destination.

After I waddled my way into the clinic, we checked in and relaxed. It took no time at all before they called my name and ushered us back into the offices that I would eventually be spending the majority of my weekends in. I was given a cup by the nurse; I was told that they would need a urine sample so they could perform a routine drug test, HIV test, and some other tests that would determine the way my delivery would turn out. I knew that because of my recent past, this was also to hold me accountable so that I wouldn't relapse.

I knew that if I made a mistake again, I wouldn't be the only one to know about it and that scared me from wanting to go back to the drugs I had been so dependent on. I weighed in, my blood pressure was checked, and then I was on my way to give a blood sample. The first appointment was supposedly the worst because all the initial testing had to be completed. I had to convince myself that it wasn't for me; it was for the baby, so that I could endure all it took to get through it.

It had been a while since I had been in a doctor's office. The last time I saw my clinical doctor was for anxiety. I knew my anxious behavior was from my drug habit, but it didn't stop me from trying to get my hands on some Xanax to take, or sell, at my choosing. My doctor had taken some blood from me that time too, and then prescribed me the medication I believed I needed, and sent me on my way. I never went back. I knew that my blood test would show the truth, my veins were flowing with the vile poison that I relied on. Now my motives were much different.

When the doctor waltzed in with a sweet smile, she announced to Tina and me that her name was Jamie. Her short blonde hair complimented her high cheek bones. The visit went by rather quickly; Tina asked a few questions, Jamie checked my ankles and did a pelvic exam, and there wasn't much she could tell us without first having the results of all the tests we had just taken. In only a few short hours we would have the results. Many fears traveled through my mind. What if the drugs I had done from before were still in my system; what if I had HIV or some other sexually transmitted disease?

After all, I had been pretty promiscuous prior to getting pregnant. All the "what if" questions did their best to make a home, until the truth of the tests were finally revealed. By God's grace alone, everything came back negative.

Jamie

Labor Day Weekend, every year, had always been a tradition in the Ward Family. The Ward Family Reunion, there- in lays many memories. This year I was sure I would have some 'exciting' news to share. However, that was not the case. In fact I didn't want to go to see the cousins 'expecting' and the sisters-in-law with their baby bumps and babies. I wanted a little baby chicken of my own to get all wrapped up in. But that wasn't the case at all.

Every year, Ben and I attend church and then book it straight to the reunion an hour and a half away, only to hang for about an hour and munch on the remnants of lunch--which we're totally fine with because the real party is at the lake house - where the close relatives hang out and enjoy each other. This year, in particular, I didn't feel like I had much to bring to the table as far as news was concerned. Anyway, as far as most of the family was concerned, I was disinterested in having babies. It was my front; I'd much rather 'pretend' I wasn't ready for kids, than share the truth that we weren't able to.

This Labor Day weekend and the following week began what, unbeknownst to me, set the stage for incredible things. This weekend is where Lesa and I can pinpoint as the "beginnings" of what God was up to. We know God's character as one that orchestrates and knows our whole lives before we even are knit together in our mother's womb. This discovery shaped me to believe, all the more, the WORDS of a righteous man prevail MUCH.

It was Sunday, September 12th, 2010. Ben and I were in church and at the end of our Lead Pastor's message; he asked us and some other families to come up to the front. He felt compelled to have the church pray over couples who were either unable to conceive or unable to carry a pregnancy to term. In the midst of wrapping up his prayer and speaking over us, he looked us square in the eye and spoke right to us. The Holy Spirit, through Pastor Chad said, "God has heard you, He will be faithful to give you a baby, your promise will be fulfilled." Looking back now, I was never told I'd be pregnant. I was told I would be given a baby.

Three days later we had youth service. During youth worship, I felt compelled to be on my knees before God; it was anointed. I felt a hand touch my back and remain there for a few short moments. Once worship was over I headed back to my seat. As I was retrieving my notebook and bible, one of my dear mentors and fellow youth workers walked up to me and said, "As strange as it sounds. Take it for what it is, but I saw you with two children. They were different in age but I saw you with two. Do with it what you will." What she spoke didn't seem foreign. It actually felt natural and, well, right.

From those moments on I sensed something brewing; it's so incredibly hard to describe. Most of my journal entries reported my contentment. I could almost see how I was spiritually nesting, as if expectant--which makes sense now when thinking about the day we would get the call. The following months my journal entries continued documenting an enlarging. There would be many a day when, as a human, I would be faithless but I felt it as more of a

healthy frustration. With the idea of adopting a baby into our family slowly becoming a reality through paperwork, I felt the strong urge to all the more intently work on my character. I wanted to make sure all my 'closets' were clean before welcoming a child in our home.

In my alone time with God I would find myself totally undeserving, thinking about all the stuff I had missed the mark on. But God remained. He stayed; even when I started confessing the bad stuff—as if He didn't already know. We would find ourselves a bit discouraged at the cost AND the time it would take AND all that would be required but we wanted it and like God, we remained.

Devotion

When we walk our life's journey it becomes much like walking a shore line. We will always encounter situations that require a choice, step out into waters of unknown depths or remain safely where we can see. *Often a safe life is a faithless life; in contrast, a life stepped out is one filled with growth, wonder and fulfillment.* A safe life produces the same safe results with no advance and no opportunity for change, abundance and miracles. God never came to make us comfortable, but courageous. It may seem scary but God sent someone to endure the challenges and afflictions with you, to help not only calm the storms around you, but in you.

Let Jesus enter the very darkest places of your heart. The places that you're afraid to let anyone go, even yourself. If you show Him into every room of your heart and invite Him into every aspect of your life, Satan has no choice but to vacate where Jesus just stepped in. There can no longer be dark where light has just entered.

Read Luke 5:1-11.

Some things to consider:

Jesus "noticed two empty boats at the water's edge." (Matthew 5:2 NLT) God takes notice - he sees our 'emptiness' and calls it opportunity.

"Stepping into one of the boats, Jesus asked Simon, its owner, to push it out into the water." (Matthew 5:3 NLT) God will always step INTO areas of your life that seem empty and vacant. While He does this He will

78

always command us to push it out.

Simon was done. He toiled all night (the prime time to catch fish) and was now washing his nets when Jesus had found them (Matthew 5:5 and 5:2). The act of washing his nets was to tend to them, in an attempt to try again later. We have to be as enduring as Simon but also willing to let Jesus in the boat. He can fish for us in seemingly impossible and impractical times.

"Now go out where it is deeper, and let down your nets to catch some fish." (Matthew 5:4 NLT. Jesus had just used the empty boat to preach to the crowds - so the crowds knew it was empty. When He commanded Simon to go out DEEPER and to cast his nets - he did it in obedience - he knew if nothing was caught, it was ultimately on God. The same is true in our lives. We need to lose our pride - go to DEEP places in our souls and trust that God will bring the net up full AND take all the credit.

Be prepared to be "awestruck" and have feelings of "unworthiness." (Matthew 5:8-9) If you allow God onto the platform of your empty boat - He will only leave you in AWE. He already knew beforehand what was to happen and already knew the condition of Simon's heart - yet He came on board anyway. He already knows us and invites himself in like a gentleman. He gives us a choice. You must trust Him and allow Him on board.

Will you allow God on the platform of your abandoned empty boat?
Do we just accept things in our life thinking that we are helpless to change them?
Do we believe God's mind is already made up and He will leave us empty?

Will you push off shore and go DEEPER with Him?

Remember He asked Simon to go out to deeper waters and remained on the boat WITH him - Jesus didn't jump ship then instruct the fishermen to be alone in the depths of his emptiness. He is saying and offering the same to you.

OCTOBER

"When we were utterly helpless, Christ came at just the right time and died for us sinners. But God showed his love for us by sending Christ to die for us while we were still sinners." ROMANS 5: 6, 8

Resa

While I sat alone at my mom's thoughts of Chase, believed to be long forgotten, reappeared. The last time I talked with him was when I told him I was pregnant and in his disbelief, all contact with him was lost. I remembered how Chase used to be logical. I thought it would be a good idea for me to go and see him. I wanted to hear what he had to say and desperately, I wanted him to quit drugs, come to Jesus, and be a family with me. To my surprise, he answered my call.

I met him at a cheap hotel to speak to him: first, about not aborting the baby, and second, about the possibility of adoption. I wanted him to agree with me, to be reasonable, and see the difference in me. Everything I wanted was just an illusion.

Chase and I ordered a pizza and continued our discussion. My sister and mom had called me a few times, left quite a few text messages and he demanded I not answer them. I secretly answered a text to my sister, telling her that I was talking with Chase and I left it at that, trying to please him, in order to get his approval for adoption. I appeared to do as he said.

"You either keep the baby and we split custody or you get an abortion. If you try to give our baby up for adoption I will fight it." Chase said bluntly. "But if we are going to kill the baby, why not give him a new life and an actual family? We aren't ready to be parents," I whispered back sheepishly, while the thought implanted itself.

My phone rang again and it was Tina. "I need to answer this." I said, "It's the lady that's interested in adopting our baby." He agreed to let me answer but insisted that I not tell her where we were. Tina was always one to ask a hundred questions and when Chase thought she was getting too nosy, he began to yell at me to hang up. "I am going to come find you." Tina insisted. When I told her that was unnecessary, the bomb blew up. I couldn't take the pressure from both Tina and Chase. She yelled at me to stay on the phone while accusing me of seeking out Chase for drugs and he yelled at me to hang up. She threatened to call the police. Then the worst thing that could have happened, happened.

Tina requested to talk to Chase. Stuck in the middle of a determined woman and stubborn man and not knowing what else to do, I handed over the phone. It quickly turned into a heated argument. He spouted off that she was crazy and that as long as he had anything to do with it, she wouldn't have the baby. I tried to silence them by taking back the phone, but he pushed me away and then stepped outside onto the breezeway, slamming the door behind him.

I listened and heard a few phrases from Chase, "Fine, go to my house, we aren't there. You're not going to find us and you certainly aren't going to get me busted because we aren't doing anything. You are crazy!" He eventually hung up on her and stormed back into the hotel room. I sat on the bed quietly and stared at him eager to know what happened.

Not saying a word about the call, he fumed as he told me I had to go with him in the morning to see his dad. He couldn't go back home and I was his ride. He made his demand and it was final. Why did I try to take things into my own hands? I shouldn't have expected him to see things the way I had. He hadn't been carrying the baby for five months, getting to know the baby. I had just wanted to convince him to give the baby up, but after this insane phone call I knew it wasn't going to happen.. The odds and his temper were against me. I wanted him to settle down so I could leave and go home. Afraid to try as he could become violent, I stayed the night. He fell asleep before me and as I lay next to him, it became another night of anguish. Sure enough, my crying eventually lulled me to sleep.

KAYLA

My sister was missing again. For the second time, Tina called my phone and asked me if I knew where she was. Lesa had been doing so well staying home and staying away from drugs. Of course that's what was going through my mind, when Lesa disappears what reason would she have other than drugs?

I called her. "Hello?" she answered. She actually picked up her phone! Maybe she's not doing drugs I thought. "Hey, where are you at?" I asked nonchalantly. I didn't want her to know that everyone was looking for her until she told me where she was. "I'm with Chase." she said.

"Where are you guys?" I asked again, this time apprehensively. As soon as she said his name, my blood pressure started to rise. At that moment I heard her talking to someone else, I assumed it was Chase. "It's okay," she said, "It's just my sister." She was explaining to him. "We are..." she had started to say when I heard a man yell and then the phone went silent.

I probably called back ten times before I started texting. Not only was I worried she was doing drugs but I was worried for her safety. I knew he was against the adoption idea and I didn't want him to hurt her or her baby. "Lesa are you ok? I don't know why you're with him but you need to call me!" I texted her; I received no response. "YOU NEED TO CALL ME NOW." I knew that no matter how many capital letters I used, she was unable to call in his company. I called Tina back. "She's with Chase!" I exclaimed, "I don't know where they are but he's angry and I am worried.

Do you know where he lives?" I would go myself and find her. "Yes, call your mom and I'll meet you guys there." she responded.

My mom and I headed downtown where Chase had a loft. We hoped she was there and this would be an easy grab, but I knew if she was at his house there would be no "easy." When we pulled into the parking lot my adrenaline was escalating. So many scenarios were running through my head. Mainly, did Chase have a weapon? I voiced my fears to my mom and Tina. In response, Tina pulled her shirt up slightly to reveal a gun. That didn't make me feel safe at all...just more worried.

We walked into the loft building and followed Tina through the stairwells. It smelled like alcohol and vomit in the halls. Beer bottles lay in the middle of the hall and outside peoples' doors. Yeah, this place screamed trouble. Tina stopped at a door with no door knob; this was Chase's loft. We knocked and pounded on the door, yelling my sister's name. I looked through the doorknob hole and tried to see inside. There was no movement. They weren't here.

We made our way out of the dingy building and decided to head home to wait for her. I was relieved no drama had happened but I was even more worried about Lesa. Where could they possibly be; what were they doing?

On the way home, I texted Lesa again. "We are at Chase's and the police are here. They are searching his apartment." Two minutes later, I got a phone call. It was Chase and he was angry. I had finally struck a nerve! "Stop lying. Why don't you go back to Stephen's? Yeah, I have seen your car there!" he

taunted knowingly. "Why don't you mind your own business and let me talk to my sister." I replied. Where is she?" "We are going to see my family. She's about to find out there's other options and a grandma that wants this baby." he replied hotly.

We exchanged a few more heated words and the conversation ended. He never let me talk to my sister. She finally did text me to tell me she was okay and not to worry. I believed she wasn't on drugs. She would have completely ignored any attempt to contact her if that's what she was doing. I thought she was dumb for going alone to meet him, but I would try to do what she said and "not worry." I relayed the information to my Mom and Tina. They didn't believe that she wasn't doing drugs despite what I said. Now it was the waiting game again. We waited for my sister to return home safely.

On our way to Chase's fathers' house, my sister called me. Afraid, I answered. Abruptly, Chase grabbed the phone and hung up on her. Upset that I was going to say something he didn't want me to say, he still wouldn't let me talk to my family. Not wanting anyone to know where we were or where we were going, he turned my phone off out of paranoia we would be tracked.

I prayed silently that he wouldn't get angry enough to hurt me. I knew that he could be kind, but I also had frequently seen his anger overtake him. In this moment, I knew it wasn't about them knowing where he was, it was about the control he wanted to have over me. I knew he felt like he was losing it; so he began to yell at me some more, to put me in my place. I grabbed my stomach showing signs of distress. I was afraid that my baby would feel the stress and want out, just like I did. I was afraid the baby would come early if I kept feeling this anxious. Chase noticed the sign and backed off just a little bit.

"Are you okay? Is the baby okay?" He asked concerned. "Yes, we are fine. My stomach is starting to hurt a bit and I just need some silence or even some music until we get to your dads," I replied. He nodded his head in agreement, the rest of the ride was silent. I could relax for the moment, but I knew it wouldn't last.

We pulled up to a large white house with a round-about driveway and a large plot of land on either side; we parked at the end of the long, paved walkway that led to the front door. Apparently, his dad had a great amount of wealth. I had known this from the beginning, but I had never seen it. Every dime Chase got from his father was spent in a very irresponsible way. Chase walked to greet his father halfway down the walkway as I sat in the car. He waved in my direction after about ten minutes and ushered me to come out. Unsure of what he and his father had been speaking about, they both stopped talking and looked at my stomach. Chase had told him that he was having a baby and that he was going to be a grandfather. Instead of inviting us in, we sat on the curb beside the car. His dad didn't seem moved, he sort of shrugged, asked a few questions, said he would help out anyway he could and wished us luck. Before we left, Chase told his dad that we would be naming the baby after him. I had told Chase that I thought the baby would be a boy and that made him all the more excited to keep the baby, IF it was his. He told me after he had mentioned it to his father that we were going to name the baby Charles.

The drive to his dad's house had lasted longer than the visit itself. I felt like I had missed out on something, before I knew it, we were back on the road. Chase insisted that I take him back and that I could just drop him off at a friend's. He was much too paranoid to go home. Thankful that his friend's house was a closer drive, I couldn't wait for him to get out of the car so I could go home too.

DebBie

I didn't have much to say when my daughter returned home. I was partially shocked that she would choose to go see him, but I also knew that it was hard for her to have this attachment, no matter how unhealthy. I had watched her fall for a man that I believed wasn't good for her. She had been doing so well. My daughter had been on the traditional path by finishing high school, going to college, and taking care of her responsibilities.

However, while she was away at college, she participated in activities that got her into trouble. She had a hard time finishing the semester and came home sooner than I expected. At home, she found a boyfriend, Chase, who was twice her age and I blamed him for taking her even further down the path she was already on--a destructive path nearly impossible to escape. I blamed him for her drug addictions. I blamed him for pushing her past the breaking point.

Scared of him tempting her back into things, I wanted my daughter to get far away from him. When she met with him my anger had already been all poured out. All I had left was heartache.

Agitated, I felt Lesa's frustration and I knew I couldn't be too hard on her even if I wanted to lock her away to protect her from the world. That wasn't an option. We chatted for a few minutes and we came to the agreement that she would be honest next time something like that happened and seek help instead of trying to do it on her own. It wasn't about how happy this made her; it was about her own safety and my peace of mind.

Lesa

Confused and looking for answers, I made an appointment with my counselor, Bridgett, whom I had previously seen for about two years. Her politeness kept me coming back and I loved that she listened non-judgmentally. Although I know that was her job, I found comfort in not being talked over. In fact, the last time I had seen her, I had been high on my desire and

I knew she could tell so she nicely "cancelled" our appointment. She was wise enough to know that I needed to be there, so she had me do an activity where I placed different figures and toys into a bucket filled with sand.

I had completed it in about an hour while she was with another client and when she walked back in I began to describe what I thought I had come up with. I believed it was pretty clever.

On one side of the box I had all things that reminded me of death: guns, snakes, poison, and drugs. At the opposite end I had all things that were beautiful: flowers, heart, keys, and locks. On the opposite side of the sand box, near the "death" end I had put a sandcastle, then a pile of rocks with sunglasses in the middle, and last but not least, on the same side as the flowers, I had put an owl.

I was pretty satisfied and it reminded me of all the options we have in life. Her interpretation was much different. She turned the sandbox around so I could perceive it the way she did. "See how you created this sand castle on the side of death. This is because if you hide, that's what you will receive. In the middle, the rocks with the sunglasses, that means you're slowly beginning to speak, to show yourself.

Last, you placed the owl next to the flowers and beautiful things. Do you know what that means?" Bridgett asked. "I just thought it was cool and wanted to place it somewhere." I replied. She smiled and answered her own question. "It means that everything is out in the open. Owls can see through the darkness. You placed this on what I see as the side of life. And if you look closely, everything is moving in the direction of new life." Not sure what any of that had meant, I left just as confused as when I had come.

As the receptionist called my name to go back into Bridgett's office, the memory vanished. Bridgett stood waiting to greet me. Instead of meeting my eyes with hers, she looked straight to my stomach. That's all I ever felt like anymore, just this pregnant stomach. I was getting bigger and more noticeable and felt like it engulfed me. Nobody saw me anymore; they saw a baby in a little girl. She quickly realized that she had been caught; she averted her eyes back to mine and embraced me in a hug. Happily, she invited me inside and we got right down to business. She was impressed at the drastic change that was apparent. I began talking about the baby, the confusion and the options I had been given. I verbalized my concerns as well as my wishes considering adoption.

"I have a lady in mind but she already has three kids and many couples have no kids. I already told her that she was going to be his mother, but I also told her I would be honest about my feelings and any doubts. I have doubts. I want a family to love me just as much as they love my baby...and I think she loves me, but I am not sure." She nodded her head, not criticizing or giving me any advice and gestured for me to continue. After some more ranting, fussing and excitement, she began to look eager. As I watched her shift in her seat I couldn't help but wonder what was on her mind. When she first spoke, she shot down the idea of finding a family that would love me just as much as the baby. "They are adopting a baby into the family, not you," she said, "don't have unrealistic expectations. Maybe read a few more books about adoption."

I gave her a look of disappointment. I would find them. I wanted to accept the truth--that the right person was out there and that God had this under control--but my faith was meager. As she noted how hurt I looked, she changed the subject.

"So, how did you do it? How did you just stop doing drugs?" "Jesus." I exuberantly replied with a large grin on my face, thinking this was a more than acceptable answer. Her smile turned crooked and I assumed she didn't understand. "Well, that's great if that works for you." She replied confirming my assumption.

Taken aback, I softly began to defend my Savior. "How is it that years of coming here, nothing in my life has gotten better, but after one night with God, I no longer have a craving for drugs, random sex and relationships, and my anger is gone?"

With nothing much left to say, the rest of the meeting filled with awkward small talk, I made up my mind to not set up any more appointments. Fully aware, I said my last goodbye to the person who I once believed gave me the relationship I craved. Jesus had taken her place.

Jamie

In the fall, we began making headway on the adoption process. We had completed the application and were saving money for our application fee. Through the prompting of a close friend, we attended a Bethany Children Services at our local library; our friends would be sharing their testimony of their own personal international adoption of their daughter. This dear friend and I had shared the heartache of not being able to conceive and had such tenderness for one another. She would sit in my chair at the salon and we would find ourselves weeping and laughing all in one visit. We would have to guard our hearts as we shared the news of our friends' pregnancies.

That friendship and the friendship full of journeys that I shared with my cousin, Megan, were evidence that God was gracing me for adoption. Looking back on all our heartache and conversation, God was working and molding a heart fit for us to be adoption equipped. Our tendency to look at the reality, rather than be still and listen to Him and His plans for us, makes me feel a bit foolish. However, He, in all His goodness made it necessary.

Ben, too, found himself emotionally involved in the process as he researched children in different countries and studied their culture. Even the act of communicating our adoption intentions to our family was evidence that Ben had embraced the idea on his own terms and in his own time; he was sold. In preparation, we began reading adoption materials and books, even our scriptural studies of being adopted through Christ our Lord.

The spiritual significance of Joseph's adoption of the baby Jesus strongly encouraged Ben. For it was by Joseph's lineage to King David, not Mary--was Jesus able to be called the true Savior--if Joseph had not been obedient to the adoption of Jesus as his earthly son, Jesus would not have been the Savior of the world promised through the descendants of King David.

What a strong encouragement and calling to all men who find it hard to embrace the idea of adopting a child. God saw adoption necessary for even the most compelling and powerful human that ever walked this Earth, Jesus Christ. Joseph was undeniably Jesus' earthly father. Thank God, Joseph's obedience removed the pride that he and any man, naturally felt toward a unique opportunity because it would come at a cost of humility.

Ben

In all that was going on, I was strongly compelled to walk the talk as a leader in my family. This season of the process had me dealing honestly with my spiritual condition. It also had me dealing with my feelings. When I began to wrestle with God like the stubborn, untrusting Jacob (Genesis 32:22-32), I was left walking differently and I could feel it. I could relate; I was more stubborn and untrusting. God was graciously wrenching it from my character. Jamie had always joked that I was an emotional robot. I didn't get overly ecstatic with new developments like Jamie did, though I could argue I was dancing on the inside.

All the adoption research gave me a new sense of adventure. I was all the more inspired and peaceful when I would meet other men who were transparent with their journey of embracing adoption and sharing their love for their adopted children. I love that God had me meet men that adopted internationally. These men laid down their pride and truly embraced children not their own despite the obvious outward appearance. I don't say that to sound ignorant, but as a man I saw an answer to a deep concerning question: "can I truly love a child that I had no hand in creating?" God, through these men, was saying a resounding, "YES," while also giving me peace that transcended what I asked and expected.

The most radical of circumstances had never happened before. A young virgin woman was pregnant; a godly man of noble character was engaged to her. Weird, unexpected, and not the way one would think the King would enter our realm of reality.

Mary probably had many plans of her own. She had a full life ahead of her. At this time in her life she was very young. In our society today, if a teenage girl is pregnant we treat them much like the world treated Mary back then.

"But people who aren't spiritual can't receive these truths from God's Spirit. It all sounds foolish to them and they can't understand it, for only those who are spiritual can understand what the Spirit means" 1 Corinthians 2:14 (NLT).

Today, in this world, the scenario would support abortion. *We are consumed with "easy" solutions and ideas that support "self" over moral convictions or the seemingly "hard."* Our natural theory is if it ruins our life--if it takes us away from our plans then we want to "take care" of it.

Although Mary may have had many fears, including rejection and death by stoning, she stayed the course. She responded to God with loyalty and obedience. Luke 1:37 says that "Nothing will be impossible with God."

Mary's response wasn't reluctant, it was certain; she was graced for it. "Behold, I am your servant of the Lord; let it be to me according to your word". Her faith accepted an unexpected circumstance that still affects our lives today. She naturally birthed the Savior of the world.

Let's not forget Joseph also had a choice to make; find a more "suitable" bride or be obedient to the calling ordained long before he even was conceived.

It's important to note that the prophecy of the coming Messiah was to be found in the lineage of David. Mary was not of that lineage; Joseph was. If Joseph hadn't adopted Jesus as his own earthly son, Jesus would not have been considered the Promised One. That's how God promised it. Joseph and Mary's obedience became a spiritual and physical battle to fight the good fight of faith. *It wasn't easy but it was done together with Him.*

"What benefit did you reap at that time from the things you are now ashamed of? Those things result in death!" Romans 6:21 (NIV)

What are you journeying that you find yourself ashamed of or hard to understand?

Are you finding yourself frustrated and wanting out - that life may be easier?

"So let's not allow ourselves to get fatigued doing good. At the right time we will harvest a good crop if we don't give up, or quit. Right now, therefore, every time we get the chance, let us work for the benefit of all, starting with the people closest to us in the community of faith" Galatians 6:9-10 (MSG).

novemBeR

6

"Search me, God, and know my heart; test my anxious thoughts." PSALMS 139:23

Another doctor's appointment was right around the corner, I was particularly anticipating this one because it would be the last ultrasound and show the baby's sex; I wanted to celebrate it. Unsure of how busy everyone else was, I really didn't want to go to this one alone. Even though the meeting with Chase didn't go as planned the first time, I decided this time I would be more assertive and try again. I had hope.

He hadn't called me at all since the month before and I was afraid he would fall off the face of the earth again. As hard as it was to keep him in my life, it was even harder to let go. I gave it minimal thought. In my mind it only made sense to invite him to the appointment. Not taking much convincing, he agreed to come, but said he might be a little late. He had to run some "errands." We both knew what that meant, but I dropped it. I was hoping for the best and was going to hold on to that hope no matter what it took.

As I pulled up to the doctor's office about ten minutes past my appointed time, Chase was already waiting for me. We walked in together and I began to day dream. This must be what it feels like to have a husband walking in with his wife, expecting their first baby. Butterflies grew in my stomach and the baby had to make room. He began kicking.

I pushed away the unrealistic feelings; my intention was not to get back with Chase to try to be a family anymore. My new intention was for him to come to the realization that we couldn't be parents. He couldn't even take care of a dog, let alone a baby! However, the appointment progressed in a way I hadn't expected.

For some reason, Chase had a power over me that I couldn't explain. I was a coward when he spoke. Most of the time, I just silently did as he said; other times, I would fight back and he would get angry. I dreaded him being angry. I used to have quite the anger issues myself; we both used to get very violent with each other. The change in me was what I wanted for him, but I didn't want to test his aggression. A few times he smiled when the cold ultrasound 'goop' made me shiver, when the anticipation built, and when the picture revealed what we both had assumed.

The baby was a boy. Chase continued to assert himself through the entirety of the appointment, telling the doctor no one was going to be taking, adopting, or aborting his baby. He was going to be the father IF this was his baby. He kept saying IF...while following all his statements with HE is the father and that HE is going to be the one to take the baby in the long run, that he would fight IF it ever came down to taking HIS baby away from HIM.

Doctor Jamie had welcomed us in as she always had. I introduced Chase as the biological father. At this point, my doctor had seen the various personalities and influences that I had been struggling with throughout my pregnancy. She had seen the opinions that each person brought to the table, believing their way for my life and my pregnancy was correct. It was as though my own voice kept getting drowned out, choked in the weeds and unable to rise. Everyone, except me, told my doctor how they planned my delivery, my choices, my due dates, my interaction, and my outcome. Although they could give birth to their objections and opinions, I knew they couldn't give birth to my child, and the choice would eventually be mine. In the midst of the clamor from all the dissonant voices, my doctor always looked at me as if to say she knew I would have the chance to talk and she wouldn't listen to any of them. She would listen to me and I would get the final decision. Politely, I thanked her when we were all finished; I couldn't believe the stress that I felt. I wasn't sure what to do. All these opinions were stuck in my head. We left, Chase satisfied and I an emotional wreck.

Susan

Sweet Lesa, friend of my son Spencer, she had floated in and out around our house for several years from dinner guest to prom date. A source of frustration for Spencer because he always saw the beauty in her that he wished she saw in herself. She was always trying to cover up insecurity with a false confidence and a restless, sometimes reckless approach to life. While a romantic relationship was not to be, they remained friends. I knew through him that she was in a dark place, sinking because of unresolved issues, drugs, and now a pregnancy.

I decided I would try to connect with her mom; I recently had begun teaching in the same building with her. Maybe I could offer some encouragement. Once upon a time, I was young, single, and expecting too.

Fast forward a week or so and Lesa was at my classroom door. She fell into my arms and I just held her for what seemed like a long time. This was new between us. She wanted to talk and we made plans for her to come by the house that very afternoon. I hardly had time to get home from work. She was there, anxious to share. Who I expected was a little girl lost and broken. Who showed up was a woman who had found her Savior.

These were not the kind of tears I had braced myself for; these were tears of joy!

Chase's words stuck in my mind. The option of parenting the little baby was heavy on my heart. Was it my gift? Was it God offering me a chance at responsibility? I let out a huge sigh and rubbed the stretched out skin on my belly that acted as a barrier between me and my baby. I took desperate breaths to release the tension I felt, the answer was too far away to grasp. Just as his words were stuck in my heart, so were my counselors. If I gave the baby up for adoption, it would be the baby being adopted, not me. Did I have unrealistic expectations? Did I not have enough information? Was I living in la-la land expecting this to all play out the way I wanted it to? More long, desperate breaths escaped from my lungs.

I had always envisioned being a mother one day, but not like this. I had wanted to have a little boy first and then a little girl. I wanted the little boy to watch over the little girl and be her protector. I had dreamt of being married, and my husband and I would have our own place. He would get me what I craved at any hour of the night and rub my back. We would have a wall with markings of how big my belly was getting. We would look forward and anticipate the baby's arrival, ready to shower him in love and admiration. This wasn't my dream. Was it selfish of me to want better, for both this baby and I, just because it wasn't the ideal way that I thought I would have my first born? I knew I was over thinking the options. Nothing gave me peace.

I grabbed a pen and empty notebook; I flipped to the first page and created a T-chart. On one side I put mothering and the other I placed adoption. I scribbled down the positives of each under the headings and then I continued to do the same for the negatives. When I was finished, I sought the answer on the page, hoping something would just jump out at me. When nothing happened, I crumbled the piece of paper and began again. As if bitten by insanity, my notebook became full of the alleged conclusions to each of the weighty options. Still, I reached no real solutions.

I watched as the ink dripped from my pen, bleeding into my paper, my hand stopped as it cramped. I tightened my grip just to realize that I could write endlessly and still never understand what I would do. How was I supposed to ultimately decide the outcome of another person when the person that I was deciding for couldn't have a single say in it? This wasn't just a decision that would affect my life, it would affect many others. What was the purpose of this war--this decision making war--tearing at my mind?

Urgency to get out of the house came crashing in like a wave. I did some of my best thinking when I was driving. I walked out to the kitchen, where my mom stood cooking ramen noodles. She was in a hurry to get finished so she could pick up my little brother from swim practice. This was the perfect chance to not only do something for my mom, but to get some alone time, away from the house, on my way to grab him.

"Hey Mom, do you care if I go grab DJ from swim practice?" I intently asked. "Sure! That would be great! Could you also grab some milk on your way home?" She smiled enthusiastically. "You bet, see you in a bit." With that, I was out the door and on my way into town. I would have at least a 20 minute drive to really search my heart. I couldn't be still. As I sat my stomach was churning. Then I heard that disembodied voice.

Even though I was sitting, I felt my knees get weak. My eyes began to stare blankly at the road before me. The lines began to melt into each other and for a moment, I felt like the world was at a halt. "You can't hear, because you can't stop thinking." The voice whispered, so closely it made me shudder. A sense of reality hit me. God was trying to speak to me and I was drowning Him out. So with a patient heart of humility, I raised one hand off the steering wheel and I asked him to speak again. There was nothing, just silence. I knew he was near, so I partially begged and boldly proposed my last questions. I surrendered my heart to hear the answer. I approached the throne in confidence.

"God, do you want me to keep him? Am I supposed to hold onto this little boy? Am I supposed to have him? Again, no answer. Now feeling a little discouraged, I persistently asked another.

"Okay God, do you want me to give him up for adoption? Am I supposed to give him away? Is he not meant for me? Less than a minute passed when all of a sudden my insides felt like they were flip flopping, my legs began shaking and the energy surged from the tip of my toes to the top of my head until I acknowledged it. The movement that I had never before felt had just confirmed the purpose, the motions that turned me inside out had tumbled into an undeniable answer.

Yes, the answer was unexpected following my discouragement and it wasn't what I wanted to hear. I had wanted God to say, "yes, he is your baby and I will make a way for him. You can keep him and we will

make it work." My ears rang with the truth; I had been waiting--some days more patiently than others--for this moment. In this moment, I heard his voice come across clearly against the grain of the world.

The mentor at the local pregnancy facility had told me that "nothing is certain." These words had remained in my mind. It seemed as though they were colliding with all the other spoken words from the opinionated mouths of everyone. I was prepared to wipe all these phrases from my mind in order to trust the Word of God, which was easier said than done.

I was preparing to make the ultimate decision. The baby would be given up for adoption. However, I felt as though I made it full circle back to square one. A whole new set of questions were beginning to arise in me but, this time, I would put the lists away and focus on God, knowing that I would only torment myself if I didn't trust that only He knew the direction for me. Everything else seemed to tangle me up in a knot and forget to untie me. I was ready to not be forgotten, I was ready to accept that God did have a purpose for this baby and, in due time, for me.

I found myself being given the grace to trust God with the emotional side of my husband. What I had learned most during this and the following months was my heart toward my husband and our marriage. We were unified and our values of family shifted back to how we were commanded, in scripture, to value each other.

I had to trust God with my thoughts toward my husband in times of frustration. I was "all in" all the time; Ben is and has always been the stable process, gradual leader. I would be all excited about developing news and occupying myself with baby registry to do's and Ben would be subtle in his excitement and fill his time with the usual sports updates. I would get frustrated that he wasn't "getting it." I took it as him being thoughtless and unfit to take on the role of a father, when quite the opposite was true. God would train my heart and mind to embrace and cherish my husband's approach to all of it. I see now how necessary Ben's stable character was and I am grateful that God didn't answer all my frustrated prayers.

It became prevalent to guard my unity with my husband. We began praying on the armor of God daily so that we could stand firm. This caused me to think of our marriage in a whole new light. There was nothing more saddening and emasculating to our husbands and future children than when adoption planning or biological children become paramount over our spouses. It can be detrimental to the life of our marriages and the life of our children's marriages! Children do not come before a healthy marriage. A

broken marriage lacking unity is no place for an adopted child. Adopted children, at some point or another, will have to embrace their identity; having parents that love and adore each other would make this season of "self-discovery" so much easier. Our hearts' yearning for children must first be something that we both want and must be something that will add to the current family dynamic, not destroy or "fix" it. Ben and my commitment was to be first to embrace and kiss when arriving home and we had made similar commitments, through God's direction and grace, before our child ever arrived. The ultimate vision was that our child would know the value of marriage.

During this time, Ben and I took personality assessments and continued to read team building books. We had a life coach that drew out our strengths so we could see them in relation to real life events. This allowed me to see the 'why's' to all the actions I was doing and for me to see all the stability, foundation and even the logical thinking I needed from Ben to keep me grounded. This appreciation, though slow and very frustrating, made the woman in me feel safe in the arms of my husband's authority and leadership.

Marriage is hard, trying, difficult, and sometimes, I think, a cruel joke that God ordained. Adding souls to that dynamic is a huge and weighty honor. I believe the health of our marriages and the homes we allow children to enter into can encourage or hinder their view of God's heart and His Kingdom.

"The heart of man plans his way, but the Lord establishes his steps." Proverbs 16:9 (ESV)

The beauty of life is there is so much out there for humanity to journey through. It makes it hard when God gives us a promise and tells us to wait. In our flesh we can easily find ways to rush the process of receiving the promise. Through this we can develop unnecessary ties to things God will eventually ask us to separate from. When we create a way to gain the promise, it's to benefit ourselves, but God's promises are to benefit many. We rob ourselves of opportunities for our character to grow when we think we have the ability to fully produce the promise in our timing.

When I (Lesa) was a "baby" in the faith, in every aspect I heard God and what He wanted from me. During pregnancy, God said, "Adoption." When I began looking for a job, God said, "I will show you." Both answers I received. Both promises he spoke to me. I trusted the words but I didn't trust that He took care of the details and was ignorant enough to believe that was my job. I didn't understand how He operated and, when learning His character, I also struggled with trusting He would follow through.

In an effort to "help" God, I went out of my way and expended a ton of energy doing what I thought was practical. In the process I found myself opening doors that shouldn't be opened, climbing through windows I shouldn't climb through and jumping over obstacles that weren't meant for me to jump over...all because I wanted results and things to make sense.

I wrestled with what was my "part to play" and what was God's. So I chased after it and in doing so, I applied with adoption agencies, talked recklessly about where I believed the baby should end up and gave a family a lofty promise that wasn't mine to give. I truly believed I was going the right way until each and every avenue turned into a dead end; many were hurt rather than benefitted in the process.

It was much like Abram and Sarai (Genesis 15-21). God had come to them offering them a promise. He promised them that they would have a son, yet both of them were growing older and older and nothing was happening. So they decided to take matters into their own hands. Upon Sarai's suggestion Abram sleeps with Hagar, Sarai's handmaiden and she becomes pregnant - giving birth to a son. Thinking that this was God's heir, they believed they had fulfilled God's promise...that is until Sarah got pregnant. It was God and God alone that provided the promise.

The choices that they made created chaos in what should have been a perfect promise. Disgruntled with their mistake, Sarai, now Sarah (see Genesis 17:15), asks her husband to rid the family of their mistake. Hagar and Ishmael were sent away by Abram, now Abraham (see Genesis 17:5). He had to pay for the choices of trying to do what God said He would do. He had tried to take God's position and paid a high price.

What is it that God is telling you to wait for?

Do you believe that God is going to follow through on His promise?

Read Hebrews 11:32-40. Are we willing to endure

the very worst in confidence that God would offer the very best?

While we walk with God in faith, many trials will come our way. We will endure many afflictions. Why? Because He desires for us to be strengthened in character and in trust. It's our obedience to His promises that show our faith. Although sometimes we may try to take on the role of God and fulfill His promise our way, *God's promise will always be kept in the way He intended to keep it.*

"Our great desire is that you will keep on loving others as long as life lasts, in order to make certain that what you hope for will come true. Then you will not become spiritually dull and indifferent. Instead, you will follow the example of those who are going to inherit God's promises because of their faith and endurance." Hebrews 6:11-12 (NLT)

DECEMBER

"Better is a little with righteousness than great revenues with injustice."

PROVERBS 16:8

The decision became real as it left my tongue and floated softly to the ears of others. Not many would know unless they were close to me. Many people, including Tina, figured the adoption with her was the answer. I still had an uneasy feeling about Tina adopting the baby.

I was growing really attached to the baby and I decided that I would call him Charlie, taking into account the name Chase had given him. It was much cuter than the name Charles, and it kept me connected to Chase even though he wasn't around. That much I needed. I looked down at my stomach and gave it a pat, soothing his kicking tantrum. "There, there baby Charlie. We will figure it out. I know that I am not supposed to raise you. I want to keep you because I love you, but God's got a plan for you. He told me so."

As I thought about how I needed to be honest with Tina, since I had told her from the beginning that I would be, I decided to meet her. I dreaded telling her what I thought; I knew it would hurt her. I knew she wanted another baby more than anything. She had told me once before that she was purposed for motherhood.

I sat in my car in front of a small local deli we were meeting at for sandwiches and tea. I had to be strong and tell her the truth. After I rehearsed it a few times in front of my rearview mirror, I realized how terrible the truth sounded. "Tina, I am so sorry. My mind isn't made up yet. I am having a hard time coping with giving up baby Charlie and I am thinking that, maybe it's because I don't believe he's going to the right family." No, no, no. I couldn't say that! I would break her heart, she would question me by saying "what do you mean, we aren't the right family?" I know she was a great mom, so how could I tell her that I didn't want her to mother my child. I wasn't at peace. She pulled up right next to me, a big smile on her face as she was waving, and my heart sank. I wasn't ready for this confrontational conversation.

Slowly, I slid my way from my car and gave a fake smile back in Tina's direction. I was a mess. My hair was wild and out of control, my clothes too tight, and my teeth had yet to be brushed. I truly did not want to leave the house; my appearance mirrored how I felt.

We sat down and Tina began to explain to me all the things she was doing in preparation for the baby. She had taken a little bag to her daughter's school and asked her to open the pink or blue bag. In each bag she had a little shoe to suggest that they were having a baby and that her daughter should be prepared for another little girl or boy to enter the house. Despite her efforts to get her family involved, they never seemed really interested. They were already a family of five. As much as Tina wanted this, her family was having a hard time adjusting to the possibility of having a new baby in the house. This also weighed heavily on the decision that I was making.

After I let her tell me all the plans and exciting news, I had to tell her. I couldn't let it go on. "Tina, I have something to say, it's important. I told you that I would be honest with you, and well... I am having a hard time letting the baby go." To you, I thought in my head, and then continued, "I have been battling with the decision of keeping the baby or having the baby be adopted. I think I want to keep the baby, but I am not sure."

I was lying. Why was I lying? I came here to be honest, but I couldn't be. I questioned in my head if keeping the baby was a more understandable outcome than telling her I was considering finding another family, but the damage had already been done. I thought at least now, this way, she would think I was keeping the baby and I wouldn't have to have any other talks with her. I wanted to just run away.

She looked at me, disappointed. The excitement burning in her eyes had just blown out. Tina looked shocked that I might even be having these feelings. Why would she not accept the fact that I was attached to my baby? These feelings were bound to happen. The truth was, I did want to keep baby Charlie...but the real truth was I didn't want her to have him. I thought I had been clear.

Not saying much the rest of the meal, she stormed off angrily. Broken and confused, I carried myself back to my car, slamming the door between me and the outside world and drove home to my hiding place.

After a couple days, I couldn't stop wondering if I did the right thing. I needed more information about adoption. What was the next step? If God wanted this baby to be adopted, why did he take away the one option I had chosen? I didn't understand.

I remembered that I had a mentor at the local pregnancy facility so, I made an appointment. She set up an appointment to talk to a woman who had a baby and was going to school. She was an example of how a single mom lives and that possibility, if that were to be my choice.

Unfortunately, I didn't want to let another family down with a wishy-washy decision. I was scared that

it might happen again; I would raise a hope and then crush it. Fear told me that I would be willing to give him up, but then change my mind and break another family's heart; it was just safer if I didn't go through that again. Taking a step was all I could do, whether or not it was in the right direction. I couldn't just stand and let fear cripple me. Fear would not be victorious, God would.

Faster than I could say hello, the secretary was welcoming me and swamped me in adoption agency pamphlets, all the while applauding my choice. I wanted to applaud the choice too, but I was still grieving the answer. I saw the faces on each of the pamphlets displaying complete happiness. These people had been blessed with a child, their promise had been fulfilled. I could see their readiness. I wanted to be them; I wanted to be ready. That night, I looked through the pamphlets and did some research. There were so many agencies, so many promises, and so many choices. All of them were for a wonderful cause, to unite an orphan with parents, but none felt right. There was one agency that stuck out to me. A lot of them were Christian-based which was the most important to me; but, this one had a picture of baby Moses. Baby Moses was my inspiration; his mother had given him up for adoption and he became a great man. It motivated me to keep trusting. They were my decision and they'd receive my call.

Susan

Over the next several months Lesa and I grew closer and closer. I was relishing being "Mama Susan" and would be lying if I said the prospect of becoming "Grandma Susan" wasn't tugging at my heart strings. But there were tough choices for my girl on the horizon and time was ticking away.

Sometimes it's hard to differentiate patience from procrastination. I was with her when she met the adoption counselor, but things just didn't seem to click into place. Tick . Tick. Tick. Will she be able to follow through with her plan of adoption if she brings the baby home, has more time to bond? The days are speeding by. We prayed for the answer. God is faithful.

Lesa

In great need of a night out, I was excited to be joining Susan and her son Spencer at a Toby Mac Concert. Susan was like a second mother to me; Spencer had also been a close friend for as long as I could remember. I had no idea what was in store. I had been to a few churches and surrounded myself with local Christians to fulfill my craving for God; it was getting mentally exhausting. I knew I loved Jesus, but I just didn't fit in. Many of them looked at me as if I were out of place. I was 7 months pregnant and single with an "unforgivable" past. Every time I would raise my hands to praise the One who gave me life, I was judgmentally stared at. I was praying that this concert would be different, much different.

The opening band was Skillet; they were amazing. A beautiful song came over the speakers, speaking not only to my ears, but to my heart; it was called LUCY. The song was about a young woman, who found herself unexpectedly pregnant and decided to get an abortion. The after effects of her decision haunted her. She knew she had to do something, so she gave the aborted baby a name. By giving the baby a name, Lucy, she could put it on the grave stone and grieve so she could move on. Halfway through, I was crying so hard.

Susan reached over and hugged me. I felt like she was proud of me for giving this baby life. I was proud of me. Finally, I made the right decision; finally I could move forward just like the girl in the song. My tears turned into whimpers as the band was finishing up their segment and getting prepared for Toby Mac's performance.

I could hardly contain my excitement. Toby Mac had been one of the first Christian artists I had heard and the song 'City on our Knees' literally left me on my knees. It talks about two worlds ,the sinners and the saints, colliding. I was very much a sinner; I wanted so bad to be better. The chorus came on and Toby Mac sang, "Love will fall to the earth like a crashing wave...." As soon as the words reached my heart, I felt the love I had felt the night I met Jesus. There was power in the concert and energy moved through the crowd. No one looked at me strangely for raising my hands. I could tell the love was overpowering anyone's desire to judge, or point fingers! It was indescribable.

Baby Charlie was dancing too. He pushed, kicked, and bobbed against my ribcage. I held my baby by cradling my stomach with both of my arms; I swayed back and forth to the music. There was nothing I loved more than praising the One who saved both of us.

Without warning, just like always, God's voice came speaking to me, "don't be surprised when you marry a performer like Toby Mac one day." I smiled politely because I didn't believe Him, but it was a nice thought.

The concert was over too soon, but the time was some of the best I ever spent. I had laughed, cried, and been so in love throughout the whole concert with the One Who brought me there, Jesus. Susan and Spencer started to walk down the center aisle of chairs before me. We ventured down to the main floor where Spencer had seen one of his friends. I tried not to pay attention, but his friend was really attractive. I did not want to look after spending a wonderful evening with

Jesus; my eyes shouldn't be wandering to anything else. I didn't need to date and even if I wanted to, I was far too pregnant to look attractive to any male my age. I didn't have a chance, but that didn't keep my mind from wandering.

What if this man is the one I could maybe date? He could like baby Charlie and then we could be a family! Yes, that could work. Then I could forget this whole adoption thing and my life's Rubik's cube would be solved. If only it was that easy. I pushed back the initial response because I knew it wasn't right. I felt awkward so I kept talking at a minimum with Spencer and his friend who he introduced to me as 'Austin'. He gave me butterflies, but I caught all the unwanted flutters and I locked them in a cage so I could focus on the task at hand.

austin

Mom had talked me into seeing this rapper named Toby Mac. Though I didn't know any of his songs; I knew that she and I had been walking in a tough season and it would be good for us to get out and take in a new experience. She got off work and we went out to eat before the concert. I was only thinking about how I hoped someday God would use me in the same medium to reach others. As we arrived at the Shrine I felt some giddy excitement knowing that a couple of close friends would be there as well! The show started right after we got to our seats. The act was very high energy and Toby was actually legit. Later on I took mom over to meet the people I had been hanging out with. My buddy Lance was down on the dance floor looking to get as crazy and close to the action as allowed, introductions were made and then it was off to the last set of friends.

My friend Spencer was very much like me, it seems that our mothers knew us very well and had talked us into joining them for a "date" night of sorts. The only difference is they had one extra person with them that night. She was someone I had maybe talked with three or so times; I had always thought she was very cute and also known as very wild. This time she was pregnant. I was actually broken-hearted when I saw her because she looked like she would pop at any moment and I knew that this baby would be born out of wedlock. We said good bye giving everyone a hug not thinking anything of it as I usually give love to those I know. Little did I know, God had just introduced me to my future wife.

Ben

In all my years of knowing Jamie, Christmas was truly one of her favorite holidays (second to Valentine's Day). It was 'snowy season' and the woman loved snow. We are both planners, though I tend to fly by the seat of my pants. Having kids and planning for them was one thing we always did as a couple.

At the beginning of the year we journeyed through many emotions. We went from trying a few last times to get pregnant, to opening our hearts...well my heart...to adoption, to applying with an agency, to waiting...all the while believing we were going to have a child or the news of one by Christmas. My heart would ache as I saw my bride weep in our bedroom or hear her in the shower. I felt like I had failed her. Nothing I could buy her would heal the deep open wound. We were inadequate in the 'baby making' department. I really loved the 'practice' but that was all it seemed to be. It hurt that sometimes it even felt emotionless and mechanical. IT made me feel unnecessary.

I would relate to Sarai and Abram (Genesis 16) and even Jacob and his wives, Leah and Rachel (Genesis 30). At this point we were willing to try anything--not necessarily resort to polygamy or bring in another option--but we can't pretend that we aren't able to relate to their hurt and above their fleshly attempts at a solution. My heart broke because, unlike Isaac, my prayers for my wife to become pregnant didn't find their way to fulfillment. I did feel the Word gave me people like them to relate to as they waited twenty years for a child, only to have twins.

My wife was Hannah-pleading before the Father. I would come into the living room and find her on her knees begging for hope or at least that the dream would relent. Would God give us a break? Could He remove this Dream? My heart would become stone at the thought of a generous Father inclining His ears to everyone but us. I was now becoming a full time Youth Pastor, so some of my dreams were coming true. That's where I remained thankful; my heart jumped from bitterness to gratefulness a lot easier than Jamie's. This truth hurt me; I hated that she was so hard on herself.

JAMie

I felt a sense of total defeat. This year was several years in the making. When we first began trying to become pregnant this was the Christmas we had planned to be pregnant with our second child. After a few years of no pregnancy successes, this had become the one we would start to hear about our first child through adoption. My outward appearance and character reflected my inward emotions. I was clearly unhappy. Ben was better than me; however, during our times alone, we were broken.

We spent a lot of money on Christmas gifts, money intended for a nursery and spoiling our first born. We had Christmas with our families and I refused to talk to anyone but our cousin Megan. She too didn't understand why God was giving everyone else children, even friends and family that weren't trying.

My sweet husband was a buffer from all my disdain and reluctance. I was awful and just wanted to curl up in my bed and eat my feelings; on my days off, I did. Warm cookies and cold milk were a large part of my diet. God found no warm welcome in my heart this month. I was undoubtedly the most bitter I had ever been in my entire life. I was certain, if it was unclear before, God hated me. He existed alright, but I felt totally forsaken. I felt that way because I chose not to squash those lies with any sort of truth. I skipped church by sitting in Ben's office during services; I didn't show up for youth services, scheduling to work at the salon instead and my Bible remained shut.

My cousin Megan, with the simplest words to share

her heart, convicted me to the inner most parts. Though we found ourselves at the dining table weeping about our obvious injustice, while others laughed in the divided living room, she still found herself praising a worthy Father. What! We prayed; my heart repented. Immediately the rush of memories flooded my mind-- those times I was at youth conferences and on my knees worshipping, saying "Just give me Jesus" and "You are all I need" and "I lay it down at your feet." All of it became real.

December 28th, 2010 I wrote a journal entry.

"...In a few days it will be a New Year. My resolution starting NOW: I will live a life that, through any circumstance, will find myself HONORING the KING. In all I do and experience-- I WILL HONOR YOU."

Devotion   Read 1 Samuel 1:1-28

Hannah's situation of wanting to be a mother went from difficult to impossible when God had closed her womb. It wasn't Satan who had made her infertile, it was God. Hannah wasn't the first woman in the Old Testament who couldn't bear children on her own. There was Sarah, Rebekah, Rachel, and the mother of Samson. The sorrows of these women were great. The many tears cried cannot be numbered or even justified through mere acknowledgement. However, all these women who had been unable to conceive were used by God. Eventually they did become pregnant in His timing and at His say so.

Trust when God delays something you want, He has something in store far better for you than you could ever imagine. He wants you to pray to Him with the faith that you will receive. If you lack faith and you complain through your suffering--all while God is trying to give you a miracle--you ruin for yourself the grace God is attempting to show you. There is a reason behind everything, however an explanation isn't always owed to us; that's the sovereignty of God. *If God isn't meeting your expectations, it's very likely He may instead EXCEED them!*

Guard your heart in the waiting seasons. Be diligent and stand guard. We love what Ephesians 6:10-14(a) says.

"Finally, be strong in the Lord and in his mighty power. Put on the full armor of God, so that you can take your stand against the devil's schemes. For our struggle is not against flesh and blood, but against the rulers, against the authorities, against the powers of this dark world and against the spiritual forces of evil in the heavenly realms. Therefore put on the full armor of God, so that when the day of evil comes, you may be able to STAND YOUR GROUND, and after you have done everything, to STAND. STAND firm then..." (emphasis added)

Though it was the Lord that closed the wombs - it is still the Enemy that perverts the heart. Don't let the Enemy undermine God's miracles for your life; God will do the miraculous. When He does, be a faithful servant ready to receive appropriately. Understand whatever you are going through, whatever the suffering, let it cause you to praise and look to God in faithful prayers--just like Hannah did. If God can restore her, He can, in turn, do it for you. In your waiting, oh lovely one, STAND.

JANUARY 8

If we are faithless, He remains faithful—for he cannot deny himself. 2 TIMOTHY 2:13

My birthday was approaching and I would soon be 20. No longer 19 and pregnant; for some reason, the happiness that came with no longer being a pregnant teen was exciting. My mother had planned to have a small gathering on a night we weren't so busy. Between figuring out adoption plans, my attention to my new found love of praise and worship, concerts and her work, both of us were hardly home.

Nevertheless, we found an hour of time where everyone would be free and we could eat cake and open presents. It was a wonderful time and probably my best birthday. My stomach had grown so much, it looked like I was harboring a watermelon, and my baby loved sweets. My little brother had picked out the funniest cake and was my favorite ever received. It was a tiny little green monster and perfect for all of us to have a small piece. I loved every minute of our time together. Family was becoming more and more important, something I had never cherished before.

As I thought of families, it took me back to the situation I couldn't sweep under the rug anymore. I had called the adoption agency chosen the month before and the scheduled meeting was quickly approaching. I knew the clock was ticking. I had less than a month before baby Charlie would be here.

Not a second wasted, the day came to meet with the agency's representative. She introduced herself as Margaret and we started immediately talking baby logistics. My due date was Valentine's Day, February 14th. I began spilling about my background, my past— the good and bad choices—until I was an empty cup.

She knew my situation was urgent and the need to pick a family was going to have to be fast. I wanted an open adoption so I expressed my concerns to her and let her know my wishes. She shook her head doubtfully and proceeded to tell me that because of my past--and the fact that the father was an ex-convict--the best she could do was a semi-open adoption, where they could send me pictures but have no contact with me. The other option of course, one she strongly encouraged, was a closed adoption where I wouldn't be able to see the baby at all. Those were the only options I was given.

He was going to be born in less than a month. If I was going to be realistic with myself, again, I believed I had no other choice and this was the only way. I began to sign off on papers; my heart cringed with each signature written. As we sat doing paper work, she began to tell me all the families she knew would be thrilled to adopt a new born baby. She smiled as she spoke and I kept a pretend smile on my face while I felt my soul was being stomped on.

Before I left, she gave me a bundle family profiles; I had to choose one by the end of the week. The family I would choose had to have time to prepare for a newborn baby, to get their funds together, and to do their side of the legal paperwork; I also needed time to prepare, prepare mentally for the giving up of my baby. I thanked Margaret for all of her help. I gave her my word that I would make the decision by the end of the week.

As I made my way home, I went straight to my room and stuck the folders right next to my bed. I planned to go through them that night, but more than anything I wanted to put it off. It was emotionally draining. I couldn't imagine their stories--their faces-- and then a choice that would change everything about the lives that they knew. Just as I was going to be looking at the many faces, the faces would be looking back at me with hopeful eyes, silently pleading for me to pick them.

An apprehensive feeling tugged at my heart, choosing to overcome it, I gained enough courage to read the first folder. The family couldn't have any children. The mother was a teacher and the father was a pastor. They loved children so much. They believed they would be blessed with one. I continued to read 20 more profiles, similar to the first. Different faces, occupations, religions, and relationships, but all of them shared the one thing that I had--the need to get pregnant, the need to have a baby. I slowly closed the last one as tears began to stream down my face. I couldn't stand to look at any more. They were all hopeless, yet hopeful. Why did I have what they couldn't? The tears turned into sobs and my soul began to ache.

As I thought about how there were many orphans in the world and many women in need of a child to love, I began seeing the injustice that screamed from each page of the profiles. So many babies without homes, so many families, and they couldn't find each other. In my lap these folders and I could only choose one when they are all truly chosen to have a complete family, it wasn't fair!

Uncontrollable sobs continued to erupt from the very core of my heart, from the depths I did not even know were there. This grief was swallowing me whole.

It was a pain I had never felt, because it was not my pain, it was theirs. I knew what I had to do. I buried my face into my hands and I began to pray.

"God, all these orphans, all these mothers and families, why God can't they find each other? I am carrying a baby, if given the opportunity, I could provide for. How can I give up a baby when so many others need homes? Would this baby be stealing a homemade for another? God, there are babies sleeping in dirt and here I hold in my hands families with loving homes-- families waiting to embrace those babies. It's not fair God. It's just not fair."

I pulled out my notebook so I could write and release the raging emotion consuming the very essence of me; I put my pen to the page and words just busted out, freely they flowed onto the paper.

"A baby's crib empty,
A hopeful family cries,
A child sleeps in dirt,
with hopeless tears in his eyes.

A home longing for laughter.
A little one they do miss.
As a child is sleeping in dirt,
waiting on a sweet goodnight kiss.

A woman longing to carry.
A second heart she cannot conceive.
All the while a child is sleeping in dirt,
without an ear to hear his pleas.

A man hoping to play sports
with a little that makes him a father.
A child is sleeping in dirt
wishing someone would bother.

A family that feels incomplete
waiting...just waiting...
As a child is sleeping in dirt
waiting...just waiting..."

As if I had just given all my strength, I felt relief as I finished writing. My hand never stopped shaking and my heart never stopped throbbing. I placed the notebook down by my bed and slowly my tears started to dry up as I laid my head on my pillow and fell asleep with one last tear rolling down my face.

I woke up in the morning feeling defeated, still not able to pick a family. I didn't want to never be able to see him. It wasn't good enough. There had to be something better, right? I felt selfish and when that anger presented itself, I began to get angry with God for letting this happen. He told me to give up my baby, but He knew that I wouldn't be able to if I wasn't going to be able to see him. I didn't understand why God would want that!

I thought about it all afternoon until I became confused and upset. Again, I placed my face on the ground and prayed. Too distracted to really get anywhere, or say anything worth any value, God knew my heart. He knew what I desired, but it didn't matter. I still pleaded with Him, showing my distrust...wishing it wasn't in my heart. That's when I heard the garage door opening. My mom was home from work. I wiped

the tears from my face and got ready to pretend I was okay. My mom walked in and threw her stuff into the chair closest to the door. She looked directly at me and could tell my pretend face was exactly that. It wasn't fooling anyone.

I quit acknowledging her reactions and began to tell her about all the families. I was laying out my suffering because I didn't believe God could fix it and maybe she would have the answer. Someone had to have the solution. In the midst of pouring out my heart, I started to notice the glow my mom had and the smile stretched across her face. This made me angrier and I sharply asked why she was smiling when I was telling her my troubles. She opened her mouth and the words began to unfold what God had been doing while I had been angry, crying, and praying.

Danelle

My heart was always very heavy for Ben and Jamie and their desire to have a child. I would hear about other adoptions and would always hope one day that could happen for them. I knew about the cost and emotionally exhausting trials most have to go through when adopting. My husband's sister was adopted through a private party so I knew it was a possibility.

One day while I was at work I overheard another co-worker talking about how her daughter wanted to give her child up for adoption but wanted the perfect fit. My mind automatically went to Ben and Jamie. I went straight to a mutual friend and she called Jamie to get the ball rolling. This seemed impossible to my natural mind but I still felt like if this was God's will, He would make it work. It was the perfect example, for me, of God's love for us.

Ben

The New Year had brought with it new promises. This time we were going to God with what these promises were. Jeremiah 33:3 says "Ask me and I will show you great and unsearchable things." We were going to God about where we were going to emotionally invest ourselves. We were going to worship our Creator--with or without a child. We withdrew from actively pursuing adoption. We believed if God wanted us to have a child, he would provide the means to do so. So Jamie and I decided we would wait until we got our tax refund back; we would then fix up the house and pay the home study required. That is where we would take a step back and allow God to take a step in.

JaMie

On Wednesday, January 19th, Ben and I woke up early to get ready for church staff meeting. Ben hopped in the shower and I was on the toilet--hey I'm telling it how it is--for some reason I remember looking around our tiny bathroom and into the hall and thinking 'I am so blessed. I am content. Thank you Jesus, you have been so incredible to me. If it is just Ben and I for the rest of our lives, I will love you still.' I joined Ben in the shower, as I was in prime ovulation time. We continued to get ready and I snagged my phone to find we both had 8 missed calls from our pastors and a dear friend of ours. As I was checking the missed calls page my pastor called again to tell me my friend, Heather was trying to get hold of me and I needed to call her. Okay...?

I call and I'm pretty sure it didn't ring and I hear Heather on the other end panting.

"Jamie, why don't you answer your phone?"

"I'm sorry girl, what's up?"

"Well how would you feel about adopting a baby boy who is due in February?"

"What?"

"There's this woman at my work, whose daughter is pregnant and due around Valentine's...a little boy!"

"A boy"

"Yes"

"We would more than love that."

"Okay, so it's okay that I already told the woman you were interested?"

"Yes, it is more than okay, wow, a baby, a baby boy."

"I feel good about this for you guys, Jamie; this could be God's answer."

We finish our call; I set the phone down on our end table and walked into our bedroom where Ben was getting ready. I looked at him and he looked back at me..."Baby, we're going to get a baby boy." It's as if I knew that this little boy was mine. I already loved him, I already wanted him, and I already needed him with me. Ben, being the guy and the logical one, remained unmoved; he smiled and I began to explain the phone call.

We headed to church, not fazed by anything but baby boy. Before lunch I had fully registered. During lunch Ben, our friend Kari, and I were talking names. Ben and Kari had to talk me back down to reality. But I just knew - this boy was mine. Back at church I couldn't think. Was this God 'giving' me a baby? It is; I know it is.

I kept in contact with Heather throughout the day, as she asked questions to relay and to see if the birth mom could look at my Facebook page. YES! Look at whatever and PICK US! I searched for her too. I stared at the picture she took of herself and her baby belly. I loved her. It was unreal. I loved her and I loved him. Within six hours I had welcomed, into my heart, two people. I would go through our Facebook photos with a fine tooth comb, thinking 'what is she thinking about us in this one or that one?' and I would look at her pictures and wonder about her story. Heather also had told me the whole story, about how her friend, Danelle overheard Debbie mention that her daughter was going to have a baby anytime and she would be taking a few days off to be with her at the hospital, then Danelle immediately thought of us, too shy herself - she knew Heather would talk to Debbie. Talk about a divine appointment.

Emotions high, but still in Jesus and stirring for hopeful things, I didn't sleep for days. I kept wondering what she thought and when she would call us herself. I prayed like Hannah in 1 Samuel 1:10, in my anguish and from the root of my being, I yearned for this. I yearned for God's promise to me; to give me my heart's desire, to give us a child. I decided this day to fast until this baby boy, my son, was born.

I can do this. This faith, that I had no idea where it was coming from, was in me. I just knew, even with such a small phone call, this was the start of something that would be reality. I seriously knew, that I knew, that I knew. All of me wanted to be able to tell my son one day, that "when we heard about your coming - we knew and believed you were made perfectly for us". I never waivered, which was not like me at all; I felt a special kind of grace from the Lord, that's when I knew. I can confidently say I believed the whole time.

That evening I was teaching kid's church and Ben was teaching in youth. I had my phone on LOUD. Heather walked in during the middle of service, only to tell me that Lesa probably wouldn't be calling us tonight because she had to work late, but she would in the next couple of days. She also let me know that Lesa was considering going through an adoption agency. I was unconcerned...who was this person I was becoming? I was given an obstacle and it didn't faze me. I knew God had this woman bear this child for me. I was however extremely bummed she wasn't going to call until she wanted. I needed a time. I needed something from her to cling to.

So we waited. Ben, the unshakeable, kept me grounded. He was excited but needed more to stand on before considering opening his heart to it. I knew that sweet baby boy was mine; though not growing in my stomach, he was growing in my heart. I just wanted her call; I just wanted to tell her I already loved her too, not just him. I wanted her in my life. I wanted to hear her voice, the one giving my son life. The feeling was unreal and the only one who knew how I felt was Ben. I didn't want anyone else to think I was insane.

A few days passed and I had to do something! I didn't know if she had seen our social media pages yet but still every day, every hour, I would look at us as looking through her eyes. I'd jump with joy when I'd find a picture with me or Ben and one of our family's or friend's baby, surely she saw those. Hopefully she sees those. I was so critical of us. I wanted to change my profile picture a million times and replace it with a picture of me and my friend's baby who was dressed up like a giraffe, but I withstood the temptation.

Then I thought, "I have a blog. It doesn't have very many entries, however it's something. Not everyone will see it. It can just be to her." I still had to be vague. That was my solution...so I wrote.

My blog entry from January 21st:

"If this is her...who carries him...?

...I'm speechless...which if you know me...a trait I often rarely possess...

You have to be confused. I commend your desire to give him safety and peace. I admire your heart for wanting more for your son...desiring greatness for him...security, love, soundness....

I can't sit by and wonder if you will chose me...my heart races wondering what you think of me as you look at my husband and my pictures...

..I'll open my heart and take this risk because I know I can be IT for him. My husband and I we love greatly and are loved greatly...your baby boy would be connected to that love. I'm eccentric and BEN is always logical, I'm creative

and Ben's a peace maker, we're lively and energetic, we have a million people who support us... there's so much of who we are that I wouldn't mind being challenged by asking with.

...I can't carry him or anyone for that matter...but we want... and we desire to love big...and to have lots to love in the future..

I'm trying to be vague. And I don't want to scare you away. But this risk is worth it to me. Many aren't willing to risk love for fear that their heart will be broken in the process...it's worth it for me... to risk. To go out on a limb..."

I reread it a thousand and one times, and Ben proof read it for me. We looked at each other, smiled, and with tears in our eyes...I pressed 'upload'. I then told Heather she could tell Lesa I had written solely to her and she was welcome to read at her convenience. I went to bed, exhausted. I slept so good, thankful; I had a full day at work waiting for me. I woke up, even more thankful that my busy day would keep my mind off the yearning and my eyes off my phone. I anticipated her call anyway.

Resa

Three days slowly dragged by as I thought about the family my mom had told me about. It was three days of decision making without meeting or hearing from them. The first day, Jan 19th, was when my mother gave me a new hope...a hope in them. The second day, the hardest of the three was the day I had to meet with Margaret to tell her what I thought. She had to know if I chose a family or not; I had reached my deadline.

With a bundle of heartbroken families that I held dear to my own heart, I called Margaret. She sounded excited--ready for what I had to say--or so she thought. I couldn't let her down over the phone, so I half-heartedly, and rather nervously, asked her to stop by my mom's so we could talk. She pulled up only an hour later. I had still been holding onto the bundle of families, scared to let them go. "What if I was supposed to pick one of them? What if I let go and it takes away someone's hope? As long as I hold on to these families and I don't make a decision, they still have hope. Right?" I thought to myself.

But, as I saw Margaret climb out of her car and head toward my door, I felt something leading me. I was not the one reaching for the knob, opening the door, and handing the bundle to Margaret. I was not the one asking her to leave quickly before I took them all back. I was not the one telling her I didn't need her help anymore but thanking her for the help she had provided. I was not the one with this kind of faith. Moments later, she was walking away, just as quickly as she had come. It was then I realized even more that the family I heard about had to be the ones because now every other door was closed except for the one concealing their hearts.

The third day, I knew God wasn't going to let me fall. It wasn't that I couldn't pick a family, it was that He wanted to...it was that He already had one in mind. God chose for me. This was the day my mom told me Jamie wrote a blog entry to me. It started out that she cared enough about me to personally write me and this scared me. It's what I had wanted the whole time. Someone who would not only care about the baby I was carrying but genuinely care about me as a person. Jamie and Ben. Ben and Jamie. I repeated it constantly in my head, falling more in love with them with every part of me.

I couldn't wait to read the blog...the blog written just for me. I sat down expectantly and looked at the words that had been typed. As I was reading I felt the Spirit all around me and it confirmed what I already knew. This was THEM. I read the blog at least seven times. Through smiles and tears I sputtered, "Mom, call them. I want to meet them. She is perfect." Without a second to waste, my mom got their number and called.

JAMIE

I was so busy I needed an assistant. I was relieved I would have extra hands in case the phone in my back pocket went off. I began to blow dry my last client with the help of my assistant when my butt vibrated... My heart skipped a beat, the kind where you get cold really fast then warm in your cheeks.

I slipped away, not caring if I was unnoticed or not. It was a number I did not have saved. The first room I got to was the break room, where girls I worked with were joking and hanging out. In a hurry to not let it go to voicemail, I answered the phone. It was Lesa's mother. Oh my gosh, it was Lesa's mother! With one hand holding my phone to one ear and one hand covering my other... unbeknownst to me, I'm deaf in that ear, I listened. Lesa's mother explained who she was and that she and Lesa would like to meet us. She asked where and when we could meet...I threw out some suggestions. I could hear HER, Lesa, talking to her mother. I couldn't breathe. I started to tear up. For a moment, I forgot where I was and realized the room had become silent and my coworkers looked concerned. My concern was with Lesa, not with my current surroundings. I held it together long enough to get a date, time and place. We would meet tomorrow, after church at an eatery. I thanked her and said goodbye.

I had to process this alone, however I had some explaining to do. I briefly shared and as I got deer in headlight looks, I headed to the bathroom to process. As I shut the bathroom door behind me, I slumped to the floor and wept like a baby. I couldn't believe this was happening. I was so grateful. All I remember saying was "God, You are so ridiculously good...." I believed Him, I saw Him differently; He was for me. I was changed and I hadn't even held my promise yet. I possessed an incredible HOPE.

After I gathered my bearings, I called Ben. That evening we went to our friend's house. I didn't eat; I was determined to see my fast through. I drank water, and prayed like a mad woman in my head, while appearing sane and naturally excited on the outside. All I knew was I had a son, growing in a woman I loved dearly, both strangers--but so familiar to me at the same time. God was doing something miraculous and I was privileged to be a part of it.

Resa

I sat next to my mom while she chatted on the phone; I had no idea what they were saying. I could just HEAR my mom talking, but I couldn't make out the words. I just saw her mouth moving and I felt like the room was in slow motion. I anticipated meeting them. I thought, "let's just go right now. Can they meet us today? I can't get ready that fast, but I will try. Is this them?"

My mom hung up the phone and I sat in eagerness staring at her. "We are going to meet them tomorrow." She responded to my outward emotion, "Until then, why don't you check out their Facebook pages?" The first impression I got was from the blog. It didn't have a face, it had an emotion. The emotion of a greater love, a love that surpassed all understanding--I could feel it...so when I saw their Facebooks...I could see it. Compassion, love, joy, and happiness radiated from their eyes. I looked through every picture, read every comment, making sure I wouldn't miss out on anything.

They loved each other. They loved their friends and families and in my mind, they already loved my baby boy. This was a blessing, an amazing blessing that didn't seem to make sense until this moment. I felt like I had been marching around the walls of Jericho without seeing the purpose, feeling useless but continuing in faith. I knew the walls were crashing down.

I tried to sleep that night, but it was impossible— not just because of the huge bell—but because I knew I was going to meet the family that was going to be taking care of Charlie. I looked at my belly and began to talk to him. "Baby Charlie, tomorrow we are going to meet your new mom and dad. They are going to love you so much and I can already tell you are going to be spoiled. You're lucky; you are going to know Jesus. You won't have to go through what I did. You are going to have a mom and a dad. I wouldn't let you grow up without them."

Briefly, I paused to wipe a few tears away from my eyes, continuing on, I lifted my head toward heaven. My thoughts turned into a prayer. "Baby boy, I wouldn't allow you to grow up without a dad. You need him. He's going to play sports with you. I know you like to kick." A smile crept across my face as I finished my conversation with God, "Charlie, know this...I love you and I will always love you and even if I don't get to see you, I hope you remember my voice. I hope you remember that I am doing this because I love you. I know that God is going to watch over you; He has big plans for you. Don't be scared."

At that moment, as I let out the very last word, baby Charlie quit wiggling and I felt as though he heard me. Peaceful, I wondered if it was because he knew he would be okay. The truth was that God held him and comforted him. In return, He comforted me by confirming that He would never depart from him.

JAMIE

We were up early the next morning. We didn't sleep all night, instead we talked about what we would say if asked certain questions. We gathered our bearings and made sure we were on the same page and articulated as a team, we headed to the church even earlier than usual to pray before the rest of staff got there and then we set up kids' church.

Ben led kids' worship and games during both services so I could be in worship. I needed a moment to give all that was about to happen to God. I felt His incredibly, indescribable peace all around me. I couldn't believe this was God's way, His idea of growing our family, but I was ready. So was Ben.

I just remember that this day, Ben was different. I looked at him different from any other time before. He was hopeful. He was going to be a Dad.

KAYLA

I had been hanging out a lot with a friend from work and he kept inviting me to church. I decided to go and really liked it. That Sunday morning, before we were to meet the possible future parents of my nephew, I asked Lesa if she would like to go with me. She said yes. When we got there we had a muffin and some coffee while we listened to the sermon. My friend played guitar for the youth group and I usually stayed to listen but we had to be going.

We said our goodbyes and he told Lesa good luck. When we got out to her car we realized her back taillight was broken. We laughed because she couldn't remember if it had been like that or when it could have happened. We started driving then realized something was wrong. We pulled over at the next gas station and discovered her tire was flat! I got worried because the time to meet Ben and Jamie was getting closer; we called our mom. She was on her way already and right down the road so she stopped and picked us up.

For a few days before, I had been contemplating what to say to Ben and Jamie. My mom found they were looking to adopt, from one of her friends. Lesa and I had also been talking about what she wanted to say and know from them. I made it clear from day one I wanted to meet adoptive prospects, not because I really had any decision in the matter, but because I know my mom and sister wouldn't ask everything they wanted. They wouldn't speak up if something bothered them. Basically they wouldn't get to the point. I already was sad she was giving up the baby and felt protective. I wanted everything to go smoothly and

sometimes when my mom or sister handled things there would be a lot of confusion and questions.

When we got to the eatery I didn't really know what to expect. We walked in and looked around. I don't remember exactly who saw who first but when I did see them I thought they were a great looking couple. Jamie was short with her hair up. She wore a cute outfit and Ben was a guy who just put off a gentle vibe. We sat down together and introduced ourselves.

I will admit I kind of took over the conversation, but like I said I was feeling protective of my sister and her baby. We talked about what they both wanted from the adoption and we talked about the hard things, like Lesa's drug use. "She's not just choosing you to be the parents; you're choosing her to be the mother." I said if there was even the slight chance the baby could have been affected from her drug use. Lesa started to tear up and Jamie got up and gave her a big hug. Even though I felt like I was the interrogator, I had a good feeling about them.

When we walked out of the emotional meeting I think we all had a lot on our mind. I told Lesa right away I thought they had a lot more potential than Tina I think we all knew, all felt, these would be her child's parents.

JAMIE

We got to the eatery really early. This was going to be where we would meet Lesa for the first time! We sat in our car; we peered out the window at every car that pulled up. We continued talking about how we felt and then I asked Ben to pray. We wanted to be so real-- not presenting any false pretenses.

We saw her mom pull up. I can't remember how I knew it was her. She explained Lesa and her sister were having car problems and she was going to get them. So we went inside and waited. Our hearts were beating so hard. So much I am sure the people next to us could see our veins pumping. We were silent...but eager. My face was flushed. I looked at Ben who shared the same appearance I did. Our eyes met as we both anticipated her arrival.

Lesa

My mom pulled up and I began to silently panic. I hadn't wanted her to leave the eatery because I didn't want Jamie and Ben to think we weren't coming. I got worried this first impression wouldn't be ideal. I was thinking if we were late, they wouldn't like us. I let my mind conjure up more uncertainty.

"What were they going to be like? Would they even like me? Would they think I was a bad person and not let me be around baby Charlie? Would they love him if he wasn't healthy? Would they try to make it look like they "rescued" this baby from an awful person unfit to be a mother? Why did I want them to love me when they were adopting my baby? Why did I feel the need for them to love me as if I, too, would be family? I looked out the passenger window and looked up to the sky. "I know God; my expectations are too high and unrealistic. I should trust you."

We pulled up to the eatery. This was the moment of truth--the heart turning, aching moment of truth! It seemed like the door was a million miles away through the parking lot. I wondered if they were looking out...if they saw me. Would I look okay to them? Would they see me and want to get up and leave? My insecurity told me about unspoken doubts, until we walked in and I saw them.

Then I saw her, Lesa...she was so...perfect. She waddled in and I couldn't take my eyes off her. Ben introduced us and I just stared at her. We sat in the middle; Ben and I had moved tables together while she, her mom, and her sister were ordering. I prayed under my breath the whole time. We sat waiting for them to sit down. I looked around at everyone in their Sunday morning routine....and we were making history. This day was going to be remembered and no one around us had a clue. Our heartbeats were in our ears. Then...they sat down.

She sat down with such relief. She was so little, carrying so much more than her baby. I could feel her concern, I could feel her many thoughts and I could feel her pain.   Her sister talked most of the time, dominating the conversation with what they were looking for in a mother and father and what they wanted as far as the adoption. Her mom would cut in to clarify with a more gentle approach to let us know they weren't expecting weekly visits or anything extreme. Then Lesa spoke, starting with a chuckle, as if to make the conversation light, communicating what she wanted for her baby, with such tenderness...as if not to offend anyone or scare us away.

After a series of questions were answered, such as how we felt about having an open adoption, and possible baby names--me answering the most, while still looking at Ben as to confirm it was a mutual decision. Lesa would laugh and I was just mesmerized by her strength. She then paused and asked Ben, with much seriousness, how he felt about having a kid. Ben

sat up and looking at me then turning back to her, he told her his heart. He had always wanted kids, even before me, he's totally committed and would love, more than anything, to have her baby.

As I listened to Ben, I fell more in love with him. I peered across the table and I found three other women in admiration of such an honest and strong man. I couldn't believe it, the man of few words, had just captured the hearts of women desperate for a perfect solution. I couldn't have been more proud of Ben. I couldn't say anything better. I couldn't really say anything at all after that.

After some more give and take, talking about paternity, waiving rights and more of the legal stuff, Lesa was quiet. She had one more thing to say...as if it was the worry... the thing I could feel from her the whole time.

Lesa

I knew the time had come to tell the whole story. I felt my tongue get lodged in the back of my throat. My mouth was dry and my eyes wet. A tear ran down my cheek. Softly, I spoke and looked at my mom to hide my eyes from Jamie and Ben. I rubbed my belly tenderly and I began to tell of my heartache. "What I did for the first few months--I smoked meth. This baby could be effected by what I did. I can't forgive myself if he is not okay. I don't know why I did what I did, but I couldn't stop. I was selfish, but I am sorry for what I did. I just want to know if you will still love him if he was 'special'?"

For some reason, I don't think I was just asking them to love my baby if he was special needs--I was asking them for their forgiveness. I was asking for comfort. I was asking for understanding. Their love never failed, never budged.

JAMie

I was unshakeable. I didn't blink and neither did Ben. Then Ben sat up as if to position his words with authority, only to say. "That's okay. That does not affect our desire for your child any less." Relieved, we moved to a lighter more irrelevant topic and then before I knew it, began to say our goodbyes. I had to hug her before I could walk away. I even believe I told her I'd love to give her a hug if that was okay... I embraced her. I wanted to stay forever with her. We exchanged numbers and left. We couldn't speak in the car for a moment. That just happened and it couldn't have been more perfect. God was there, I knew it, Ben knew, and she had felt it too.

Later that day I began to notice her "add request" on my social media page and her "likes" on our pictures, statuses, and such. I just kept seeking God's presence. I just wanted to be near Him and His goodness. In this season of anticipation, I felt so much joy. I felt like I was revived from a coma and I couldn't believe the life God was giving me to travel. Something was happening and we were so excited to be a part of it. God was so radical that He would consider us worthy of this calling.

The night of Jan 23, time moved slowly. I had so many things to think about. I was sure of them; Ben and Jamie were definitely the ones. It felt right, but my mind kept going over the lists I had made—over the positives and negatives of giving him up. Why did I keep looking back?

I had fear of the future. I had fear of what moving forward might look like. My biggest fear was they would divorce. What would I do if Ben and Jamie didn't stay together? I had seen so many couples fall apart. I had to face the fear upfront and tell my fear it was wrong! I knew it was better to take a chance of giving up Charlie to two parents and give him that chance of having a Dad.

A dad's role to a young developing child is so important. My dad was there for me when I was younger. He was disciplinarian and friend. He taught me most everything and I can't imagine what it would have been like growing up without him...even from when I was just a baby. After tackling my biggest concern, I dozed off in contentment.

The next morning I woke up and couldn't stop thinking about what decision I was going to make. I strolled into the kitchen where my Mom was and I asked her what her thoughts were. We talked for a little bit and shared comments about how perfect we thought Ben and Jamie were and how it would be hard to give up Charlie--but worth it. I knew I needed to meet with Jamie again, so I called her and asked if she wanted to get lunch. She said she could meet me that afternoon. I told her I would be there as soon as I dropped off my car at the shop since it still had a flat and broken tail light.

The meeting couldn't come soon enough. I was looking forward getting to know her and confirmation that this was absolutely where Charlie needed to be. I felt like I had a split personality; my flesh and my spirit (which I didn't know at the time) were fighting. One minute all would be perfect, the next, I would question all my decisions.

I dropped my car off at the shop and realized I was running behind, so asked my mom if she could drop me off at the restaurant Jamie and I were meeting for lunch. She had to go to work and wouldn't be able to pick me up. I had no idea how I was going to get home, but I knew I couldn't miss out on this opportunity.

As we pulled up, I saw that Jamie was already inside waiting on me. I was late--like always. I came up to the booth she sat in and dropped off my stuff on the opposite side. I sat down across from her and we began talking. She was polite and patient. We made small talk at first.

I needed to hear something real. She answered all my questions, no matter how seemingly insignificant they were and by doing that she showed me something no one else had--respect. She valued me as a person, not just my baby. I could see she wanted me to be just as comfortable with the adoption as I possibly could be.

JAMIE

Monday morning, January 24th, Ben and I were on an emotional high! We were working in the church office and my phone rang. It was Heather. She had found out from Lesa's mom they had loved us and wanted to pick us! What?! This is insane! But I had to hear from her. In Heather's excitement she told me, but it was more for Lesa to do herself. Honestly, if I was in Heather's shoes I would have done the same thing. Everyone was excited and wanted to be a part of the story.

Ben and I, along with our close friend Kari, went to eat where we again talked about adoption details and began to figure out baby names. I couldn't believe it. I was picking out baby names that were actually going to a baby! They were going to our baby! Our baby that was going to be born within the month! I tried not to get too excited, although that was not the case. I still needed to hear from her.

Finally, after the anticipation all morning, Lesa called. She asked if we could meet somewhere close to her mom's house. We decided on the same restaurant that I was already at with Ben and Kari, just in a different town. Go figure. I let her know Ben was going to be attending something with some youth and wouldn't be able to come. She was fine with that, so we said our goodbyes. I was sweating, but I ran all over the church dancing anyway!

I went home and showered then jumped into my best 'I'm a cool, but chill, but incredible mom' outfit. I packed my computer full of our pictures and I was off. Lesa called and let me know she was having car issues and had to wait for her mom to take her to meet me. When she arrived I gave her a hug and she went to order. When she sat back down we started short conversation. I felt the questions she was asking were more on the side of making me feel she just wanted to get to know me rather than tell me something.

As the conversation went on I began to wonder if she wasn't sure if she was going to wait a bit longer or if she was waiting for Ben to be around before she would officially say anything. She was being vague. I showed pictures of our home and what would be the baby room. She moved to my side of the booth and we shared more pictures. She then began sharing with me some things she had written in her notes section on Facebook.

She could write. I remember being close to her, not in a weird way, but the nearness of her felt right with my son in her belly… right next to me. I wanted to hug her and never let go. I wanted her to feel her worth and my gratitude through my embrace. I felt the presence of God so indescribably much. She moved back to her side and we began to talk about adoption. She told me her story from when she found out, to her first months, to the birth father, to the first family she considered for adoption and then to us. I froze, my heart missed beats.

Lesa

After talking and laughing for almost two hours, Jamie smiled real big and squished her face. I adored when she did that. Her facial expression of eagerness and excitement, while also full of gratitude, told me what she was going to ask before the words even left her mouth. Her voice became a softer, but direct tone. Then looking me straight in the eyes she asked, "Are you going to choose us? Are you going to choose me?"

I looked back at her shyly, my smile meeting hers, and I answered. "If you want him, yes, I want you two to be his parents!" She couldn't stop smiling and neither could I. I thought when I told her she would be crying. It wasn't like anything I had ever felt. It was a joyful moment, one I had never felt so much confidence in. I knew it wasn't by chance we had heard about each other!

JAMIE

I got up and practically jumped over the table between us and embraced her. I couldn't believe it but at the same time, I could. I was going to be a mother and Ben was going to be a father. God was good.

After we chatted for a bit longer she asked if I could take her to her car that was at the shop near us. I was willing to take her to the moon and back! She also extended the invite to go to the doctor's appointment with her the next day. My jaw dropped. This was all happening. This was legit. We laughed in the car and as I dropped her off, I hugged her again. I made sure she was in her car and moving before I drove off. I called Ben in tears and could tell he too was amazed and grateful. This was all happening.

Lesa and I exchanged numbers and began texting throughout the evening. We were all excited. This was developing right in front of us and we were there for the ride. It was as though this whole thing was finally rising from so much pain and hurt. Promises were being fleshed out and hope was evident. My sister came to our house that evening with a bathrobe—Paxton's first gift ever. My sister and I, with Ben's reluctant approval, headed out to get one outfit to celebrate.

Rosa

Doctor appointments were routine for me. I was going every week and at every appointment I got to embrace the sound of little baby Charlie's heartbeat. The sound was a testament to God's faithfulness. Something so wonderful and timely, something put together so brilliantly, something crafted with only the utmost care...was a second heartbeat...knitted tightly to my own. It's hard to explain the sound of something so extraordinary, the connection that grows between a mother's heart and a child's, as the mimicking continued in a harmonious symphony.

It's something that needed to be shared, although not many people could understand the *love connection*, unless they had children of their own... and even then, the closeness of an approaching separation could not be comparable to the raising of their own. I wanted to share this story with others, I had been through many guests up to this point.

After all the struggles and juggling people in and out of each appointment, there came a time to share the moment—this new life—with the mother that was going to love and cherish the heart she would hear. So I invited Jamie to come with me to partake in such an extremely miraculous appointment—the one that would give her a first listen to the baby's heart that she would nurture.

I wanted her to experience every moment she could. It was important to me that she gained the emotional, attaching bond a mother felt to her baby. I wanted her to know what it was like to be pregnant. I wanted her to have the opportunity to feel as though she and this baby were truly connected...not just in body, but in spirit. I couldn't think of a better way, then for her to hear the sound that inevitably changed my mind to choose life for him... the sound that spoke louder than any words ever could.

I had faith when she would hear, her faith would be awakened even more and the attachment would automatically synchronize. I wanted more than anything for Jamie to be pregnant. I thought how unfair it was that I could be pregnant- expectant and undeserving-when she was not expecting and deserving. I wanted her to experience every single move baby Charlie made in my stomach, the wiggles that lodged his love into my heart.

She deserved to be there every step of the way. As I was walking into the Health Clinic my brain wouldn't turn off and my emotions began to jump like jumping beans all over the place. We had been texting all morning and I couldn't wait to see her. My mother had come as well, as I wanted this to be a shared experience.

As we walked into the building, we saw Jamie sitting patiently by the window. She had a box with her and a coffee; knowing Jamie from the very few times I had seen her, I knew she was quite dependent on her coffee. These nonchalant, seemingly small traits were what made me grow more and more to love the woman who reminded me of myself I hoped because of our similar characteristics that one day, I would grow to be just like the woman she was.

JAMIE

Journal entry January 25th..."In a few hours I will be checking in to the doctor's, seeing an ultrasound, and hearing a heartbeat belonging to the baby that will be my son. God, you are Infinite! I am so small and incredibly indebted to you. Bless Lesa. Touch this baby, heal their hearts and give her all the desires of hers. Establish this relationship between us, as a deep supernatural connection. Make it unshakeable, unlike any other. Begin to teach me and mold Ben and me to be parents to this boy, shaping him, and establishing him in You. I give him to You! I love You."

I woke up early, braided my hair, and sat with a cup of coffee on my couch, Bible open, heart about to explode with gratitude. God was going to have this day. Ben was already off to work. I, myself, prepared for the day the only way I knew how, in God's presence. We talked all night about what needed to be done with the house. We prayed for provision; what we needed done would cost. Ben and I were also pretty sure on a name. We wanted a name for our son that claimed the truth of this entire miracle. Peace, God had given me a sure PEACE. So we decided that night his name would be Paxton but we'd call him Pax. Pax, in Hebrew, meant 'peace.' I prayed for him and his gifting. I prayed God would raise him up.

I couldn't believe God knew about him this whole time and that He had him for us. In less than a week we went from no children, to a boy due in a few weeks, and a relationship with an extraordinary woman. Precisely a week before, we had no clue our life would change and now I was in a humble position under a Lord who granted my truest, purest desire. Our prayers before bed every night were, "Lord you know our desire to have a child, Lord provide everything we will need, cover the logistics, cover the cost, we give this to you." We knew God would provide.

I got ready and headed out early to the second greatest gift God gave human kind under Jesus crucified, coffee. I walked in and wanted to get her everything in the coffee shop...and I nearly did. I ordered our drinks and then asked the man working if I could just have one of everything in the bakery window. He asked me how I was and, without hesitation, I told him briefly but excitedly I was going to meet my baby's birth mom to hear my son's heartbeat. I also told him it was imperative that I needed every kind of goodie for my baby mama, and one of everything was a good place to start. He chuckled and began to share the story with the girl making my coffee. They genuinely shared in my story, which only made me more excited and anxious to see her.

I found the clinic and parked. I said a prayer and texted Ben, to keep him updated. I then texted Lesa to let her know I was there and she told me where to wait. As I waited in the lobby, I watched couples, as well as women with children coming in and out. I sat across from a man and his 3-4 year old son, who ogled my box of goodies.

I got on my phone to look online for a gift to get for Lesa when she had Paxton. I racked my brain to come up with something tangible and meaningful to get to let her know I was so grateful for her.

She walked in moments later with her mom; well it

was more like waddling. Extremely grateful for my goodies, we embraced and headed downstairs to check in. My senses were heightened. Lesa checked in and her mom headed to use the restroom. We joked a bit about her need to eat all the time and how she used her belly as a table, and how the baby was as I touched her stomach.

Moments later her name was called. I helped her up and we headed in, Lesa's mom had not returned yet. When we came in, Lesa was instructed to pee in a cup left for her in the restroom. She joked it'd be easy because the baby was always on her bladder.

When she returned, we walked further down the hallway only to stop to be weighed. I wanted Lesa to know I was there for her. I took her purse and coat; she initially wanted to put them on the floor.

It hit me like an emotional freight train out of nowhere - she was doing this alone...she's been doing this alone. I'm sure she's had family and friends but it wasn't the natural course of events for a woman pregnant (in my mind) and not at all as God intended it. She wasn't coming with her husband or the father of the baby, she was coming alone. I fell in love with her even more. She stepped off the scale, seeming miserable, as she hadn't been sleeping well, but to me, she was beautiful. I locked down the tears. I was in love, with this baby and with this woman. She was so strong, yet so humble.

I continued to carry her things and made her feel ridiculous for thinking she needed to carry them herself. We walked in the first exam room. She was instructed to undress and as the room blinds were pulled, Lesa's mom rejoined us, seeming to have just gotten off the phone. Lesa had me open the blinds once she was done and we chatted while we waited. We joked about her unmatched socks and then she and her mom talked about plans for the day. I began to run my own checklists in my head about all that still needed to be done but had this confidence that all was going to be taken care of. I also really needed to tell my parents, we needed to start telling family. Other than my sister and one of Ben's cousins (who also shared in our pain of not being able to conceive), no one else really knew.

The doctor came in. I'm pretty sure I stopped breathing. I felt like at any moment I was going to wake up. Was this reality? My heartbeat was in my ears. Was this going to be a continuing occurrence? The doctor introduced herself, she also was Jamie. I joined Lesa near her head as Jamie checked her. There was going to be no ultrasound, as I was expecting.

Either way, I was honored to be there. Lesa and Jamie began to talk about birthing logistics, and when she would need to head to the hospital. Lesa introduced Jamie to me and when Jamie asked if I was a friend. I felt so privileged, especially by how Lesa did it. She was so confident, she was proud of me...of her decision in us. It was the first of many times Lesa would introduce me as the mother of her baby. Lesa then told her I would be in the room with her mom during delivery. Was this happening? We talked about it but to hear Lesa say it out loud was like making it crazy kind of weird.

After checking dilation and again joking about her mismatched socks, it was the moment of truth, more for me, anyway. I was going to hear him. It took a moment to find the heartbeat, like in slow motion. I prayed. My prayers were being heard in heaven. I could hear God whisper, "Meet your son." I was silent, making sure I heard God correctly. Any worries of the health of baby boy or Lesa's legal right to change her mind, any that were somewhere in my spirit, very quickly vanished with those words. Those words of truth and then, I heard my son's heartbeat. He's in there...inches from me. I held it in as best I could and only allowed the rims of my eyes to glisten - for those appeared before I could help myself.

Lesa

I was always ready for that part. I wished I could hear it every second of every day...the beating of my baby's heart was like a hammer beating the nail of love deeper into my own heart. Healthy and loud, like a strong wave in the sea, the heartbeat quickened but kept a perfect rhythm. This was a heart that was about to receive all the love I had ever wanted. One thing stuck with me...although the heart was loud, it was in my belly. It was free from the world. Strong and untouched, it remained hidden away from a weak, touched world. It was hard for me to imagine this strong heart ever going through heartbreak. I wanted to protect it with all I had, but then I looked at Jamie. She shined beautifully in the Lord's light.

In humility, this was the first time that I had realized I was only the planter and she was the one, chosen by God Himself, to water. I couldn't protect the heart because the heart was not going to be mine to protect. I had to relinquish control. I knew God would provide for them. I could see the joy that glimmered in her eyes. God was doing something greater than I could have ever imagined. When we heard his heartbeat, we shared the reality that lives were being changed in the world by a life that had yet to be born into it.

JAMIE

We finished the appointment with instructions on hospital bag and rescheduling. I would be returning with Lesa for her next appointment a week later, upon Lesa's eager request. We embraced again and I left to head to work. On the way I called Ben with details but he couldn't talk until his break. I parked and like a stopped up dam, I bawled. Lesa and I continued to text throughout the day. I was able to call Ben with details at lunch. He was excited, like any man, keeping a monotone voice, I knew he was excited but he's a guy. I knew once he held that baby, he was going to finally lose his cool.

That evening I came home. Ben had incredible news. God had provided. Insurance had sent us a check to cover ALL and MORE than we needed to fix the house. That night, exhausted, I fell asleep like a satisfied well-fed baby. In the morning, we would begin home renovations. My faith was increasing! I went to bed that night and woke up the next morning encouraged. I was able to HEAR and SEE the Lord was GOOD. God had not tuned me out. He heard every prayer Ben had prayed over us every night.

Sometimes we can make OUR WHOLE LIVES about one miracle... our thoughts, our actions, our planning, our time, our love, our energy...everything invested on one promise. God honors our heart and He also sympathizes with our weakness. But even in the midst of carrying out His will to the cross, Jesus made time to be in the presence of the Almighty. God gave us all His son that we might have access to HIM and be an HEIR of unearned promises. In our excitement and even acknowledgment that we didn't earn it we can get wrapped up in the Promise - leaving no room for glorifying the Father - the ultimate gift giver. Our small mind and human tendencies can place the PROMISE KEEPER in the back seat to the PROMISE.

Exodus 14:12; 16:3; 17:3.

While we wait we can find ourselves relating to the Israelites - complaining that we are better off being slaves to sin - in our old Egyptian lifestyle - than stuck waiting for the promise. Even saying to Moses, "Is the Lord with us or not?" Exodus 17:7.

Then, when what God has been working out all along is revealed we can again find ourselves like the Israelites, specifically Achan in Joshua 7.

The Israelites plundered their promised land (only by the help of God) and rather than offering the plunder to Him some of them kept it for themselves, as if it had more value than the one that created it all. If you have a tendency to do this - find yourself in the redemptive hands of the Father - being truly repentant, ask Him to work this out in your flesh and to train you to always remember our truest treasure is not found on Earth but is awaiting us in Heaven.

While on Earth it is necessary that we are grateful and receptive of what God entrusts to us , it should never be found in the place of where God should be in your hearts.   As we mature God will give you opportunities, victories, miracles and fulfill promises in an effort to train your mentality and to guide your worship.

Keeping your eyes on "Jesus the author and perfector of our Faith." Hebrews 12:2

He has to be the focus not what flows from Him. What flows from Him is the blessing of following Him. Being able to greatly appreciate what flows from Him only comes when we still keep our eyes on Him when we receive it. *If our eyes are planted on Him while we are receiving, we will not hinder the way we get it, the pace in which we get it, and the great value that God intended it to have.*

A prayer to pray if the promise has become more important than the promise keeper:

Lord, I do not want to delay Your promises to come because I'm too busy enveloped in a promise I received now or the attention I give to waiting for it rather than on You. I love You, LORD. Holy Spirit, train my mind and guide my heart to seek God first. Thank You for Your mercy. Thank You for Your forgiveness. Help me to keep my eyes on You and to keep willing and obedient heart for what's to come.

february

9

"I will meditate on Your majestic glorious splendor and Your wonderful miracles. Your awe-inspiring deeds will be on every tongue; I will proclaim Your greatness."

PSALM 145:5-6

JaMie

I had weeks, a couple to be factual, to get ready for a baby--a baby, not a puppy. I had already registered. Those around me were getting really excited about throwing a shower. I wanted family to start knowing! Even now this sounds so backwards to me, my friends knew, people I worked with knew, but my family didn't.

Lets' rewind for clarification: Ben and I were called to Republic, Missouri in 2008 to work at a church. Our church became our family. The people we worked with were family. Ben had relatives that were close and took a vested interest in us; however, we were mostly around people from church and work. People were always concerned we hadn't had children yet. We had a lot of people wanting to pray for us and give us faith books and magazine excerpts on people who got pregnant after proclaiming specific scriptures. People were invested all in love and deep hope we'd conceive.

Our parents didn't understand nor our extended family. No one had ever adopted before so we wanted to have details and more certainty before sharing with our parents and family. I took time during my lunch break to call my family.

I called my mother first. She was extremely confused and apprehensive. Hesitant that her daughter may get her heart broken, which inevitably would break hers. I called my dad while he was at work. He had no clue what I was talking about and said "Uh...okay." My dad is a great dad but, nevertheless, a man. I knew he'd come around when he held that baby. I then called a dear friend and family member.

Megan was married to Ben's first cousin; he was practically a brother to Ben and she practically a sister to me. They were married a few months before we were and began trying also a few months before we did. She wasn't able to become pregnant. At family gatherings, we'd sit and talk alone about our deepest desire and cry together.

Unlike me, she did the hard work of doing tests, going to the doctor, and such. She had to be tenderly told by me I was going to be given a baby before her. It was my hardest call, yet unsurprisingly, she was tender and incredible; she shared in my joy. I knew her heart; though she was excited for me, she still lacked her promise. Ben did his part to call his family. Afterwards, we blasted the news on our social network pages. Now the showers could commence.

My first shower was with girls from my salon. I worked part time and loved everyone there; however, I wasn't mega close to any of the ladies. Most of them didn't have children. They were so excited for the new addition but also were concerned about the chance that Lesa could change her mind.

Speaking of Lesa, it was really important to me that Lesa came to the showers! I wanted her to see who was going to be in our son's life and that he was going to be celebrated well!

The day of the shower I was nervous. I got there on time and no one was there. Within a few minutes I received texts letting me know that many of them would be late. Lesa arrived and we all tightly huddled into a small meeting room at the back of a coffee house. Lesa and I sat at the end of the table; I felt blessed.

Resa

I wasn't sure what to expect when I thought about the baby shower. I had no idea if I was going to feel completely out of place or if I would be welcomed. I didn't want people to have an image of me with the baby because I only wanted the baby to be seen with her. She would be the Mom and I didn't want to take any attention away from Jamie or HER baby shower.

Thinking about less serious things I contemplated on what I would even wear! I could barely fit into anything I owned, so I ended up picking out a black and white stretchy dress. Little did I know how ironic my outfit choice was.

I walked into the Coffee House and didn't see anyone. Just as I texted Jamie, I saw them. All the girls were waiting in a small, sectioned off back room. As I walked toward the room, I was so nervous. Was it going to be weird seeing things for Charlie when he wouldn't be mine? Would I be able to say things were cute without seeming as if I wanted them for myself? I didn't want to come off as though I was going to be TOO attached to him, even though I was attached. I didn't want them to think I would change my mind because I was involved in the shower. Nerves just...slowly... took over.

But then, I saw Jamie and she walked me inside. All the girls were smiling at me. They were all genuinely happy and I could feel the excitement radiating off of Jamie. I took my seat next to her and everyone began talking to each other.

Insanely enough, they all started asking me questions--asking me about how my pregnancy was going, what I liked to do, and then we all just started making jokes. I told them about how I would always waddle.... it was like when you get off a treadmill and still feel like you're walking on moving ground... when the baby would come out, I would still walk like he was in my belly! Then they made a joke that I would come in black and white because where they all worked they always HAD to wear black and white. They laughed and I took it in. Their laughter warmed my soul. It made me feel at home and so graciously welcomed.

Jamie began opening her presents. She received clothes, bedding, and tons of incredible gifts that she had registered for. I remember one in particular that had the name "Paxton" on it. They were graffiti looking little shoes--so cute! The name Paxton... was perfect. It was meant for him. It seemed to fit... As soon as I said it in my mind, I realized this was going to be PAXTON.... He would BE her PAXTON and he would bring peace to our family and to hers. He was already doing what his name was stating.

All the sudden, one of the girls got up and slid the last present on the table to me.

"Open it." They said.

"This one's for me?!" I replied.

Their smiles and eyes lit up. It made me want to cry. They went out of their way to put together a gift for me when it was my HONOR to give my son a better home, a better family, and a better life. I could not believe that they would be so kind; I wanted nothing in return. I wasn't doing anything for them, I was doing something for a little boy and for Jamie... and because they all loved Jamie so much, they accepted and loved me like a friend, like part of their family. Was this what "pure" love looked like?

The present was about seven different Paul Mitchell hair products! I was so grateful. I seriously couldn't believe all the stuff they put together. For someone to do something so nice was just overwhelming. I wanted the day to last forever. It was the first time during my pregnancy that I felt appreciated; I felt as though the right thing to do was starting to bear fruit and I was an important part of the equation. I wasn't just going to be the mother birthing this baby; I wouldn't be forgotten about and at this moment, I was loved just as much as they were going to love Paxton.

JAMIE

Within days I had another shower. Women from the church had a shower at my Pastor's house; my mom and youngest sister were going to be in attendance as well as Lesa's mom and sister. They were going to meet for the very first time.

I worked most of the day and rushed home to brush my teeth and meet my mom and sister so I could show them how to get there. We arrived. This was it, reality for my mother. Many women followed. I was honored, as any woman being celebrated. All these women came, with gifts for my son (no matter the way I was getting him) and gifts to honor Lesa. The decorations, the honor, the detail, and the cake looked incredible. I was fasting, so the cake would have to be frozen.

The only thing missing was Lesa, her mom, and sister. Soon enough, though, she found her way and entered with her mom; her sister couldn't make it. Lesa was stunning. I felt so privileged to introduce her to my mother and my younger sister, who still didn't understand, yet we were courteous.

We took some pictures, ate some cake, and made introductions when we were all seated. I was amazed at all the women that came. My mom was able to see my support system, my Republic family. I would catch her looking at me tenderly. It was becoming a reality to her.

The gifts were endless. The love was stuffing the room. Then they pulled out the huge amount of gifts for Lesa. Art supplies, journals and letters of love and thankfulness. I sat at Lesa's feet as she told me about her discomfort and lack of sleep. She was compassionate about it; being cautious to not appear ungrateful she was pregnant. I looked around the room and became overwhelmed with pride; I was so proud I had the honor to know these women. Women who showed up in such a giving and intentional way for a woman they never met, thanking her for giving their friend the greatest of gifts. They were watching a miracle. God was so good.

Lesa

It was the perfect shower filled with games and love, like one I always had dreamt of having for myself. However, it wasn't for me in the way I had expected, it was for Jamie. She gleamed beautifully as happiness danced across her face. Her friends and family were present making the atmosphere much more surreal than the first shower where it was filled with co-workers. In a sense, they too were family, but the closeness was much more apparent here.

Friends and family that had known Jamie practically her whole life looked at her with wide eyes of happiness, but the bitter-sweetness of the event was apparent. Although they knew she was receiving a baby, most of them wished she herself was pregnant and would enjoy, even the hard times, the moments that an expectant mother experienced. The kicking of the unborn baby and the various random cravings that came along with pregnancy was what made it so fun to talk about. It's what made it so relatable to other moms of the group. I was beside myself she could not have this moment all to herself; she would be sharing it with me because I was carrying him. I wanted this to be all hers.

I began thinking softly to myself how unfair it was the women couldn't play the traditional 'measure the belly' games or tease her about how big she was getting. I knew this was God working on my heart as I watched her open present after present. I delighted in the smiles she turned my way when something cute melted her heart. Celebrating, while I grieved, we both giggled and I covered my mouth in awe. Truly, I loved every moment.

As she finished with what I thought was the last present, because she still had one tucked away by the fire place, Jamie grinned the biggest she had all night, turned to grab the last present and walked my way. My heart sank, probably bopping Paxton in the head, and I held my breath. Everyone was staring at me, waiting for a reaction.

"This one's for you." Jamie said as she set the blue bag down on my lap.

The present was larger than I anticipated. Everyone, so eager to see what was inside, leaned forward. I didn't know how to react. I reached my hand inside only to pull out journal upon journal and a variety of art supplies. I felt tears coming to my eyes. This is exactly what Jamie and I had been talking about just weeks before. She had asked me how I was going to cope when giving Pax to them. I had told her I wasn't sure, but I did know I loved to write and my journals had kept me afloat. I mentioned also I would do artsy things because they seemed to take any negativity away. It would help me overcome.

I looked around the room as a tear rolled down my cheek. Jamie proceeded to tell me the women had pitched in to buy the gifts inside the bag. I was shocked; these women, which knew nothing about me but welcomed me with love and weren't afraid to be honest with me. They had considered me. They didn't have to, but they did anyway. God was showing Himself not only through Jamie, but through her friends and family.

This is what I am going to have after Pax is given

away, I thought. I won't have a baby. I won't have him to snuggle; this stuff is replacing him? I could feel my face turning red and I didn't want to ruin the baby shower with 'woe is me' feelings. I had to pull myself together. The gifts were beautiful and a blessing. I flip-flopped so often on this emotional roller-coaster.

Paxton seemed to approve of the gifts, making me forget about my grim thought just seconds ago, as he began kicking. I reached up to grab Jamie's hand; I placed it on my stomach. Not sure if it was a butt or a leg, we felt him push back. Laughing, we enjoyed the moment that Paxton gave us with his wiggly body. All the girls shined acceptance.

During my whole pregnancy I had felt as though I was seeking the acceptance of anyone who saw what I was going through or anyone that could help me. The thing about being accepted though is--once you get it-- you realize that the only One you'd truly been seeking acceptance from is God.

While attending all my showers, Ben was tackling the house. God was good to provide all that we needed. I found myself painting Pax's room two different times, finally settling on gray. Things were coming together. One day I had a few girls over for well over 15 hours, painting, cleaning, organizing and so forth. I was beyond grateful! My sister and I actually retiled my shower one afternoon and evening.

We were doing our part and God was taking care of all the details with the adoption. Ben's uncle was a lawyer and agreed to do our adoption pro bono. He was really nervous as it was not his line of law, but he strongly felt the Lord compelling him. He was unusually slow at work and knew it was God giving him time to read up on all we needed legally.

Lesa was feeling celebrated and welcomed; Ben and I were being strengthened. Strengthened by God's favor and faithfulness, by Lesa's humility, by my friend's compassion, and by my family's opportunity to see God - the One I serve that they didn't understand why I did. Even more they didn't understand why any of this was happening; He would do miracles and show Himself.

Resa

On February 8th, I had another doctor appointment. All the fun showers were over and it was time to bear down (No pun intended). Dr. Jamie wanted to see how the baby was coming along. He was due on Valentine's Day and everyone was anticipating his arrival. I was getting tired of carrying so much weight around but the wait was necessary. Little Paxton needed all the time he could to develop and grow.

I asked my Mom and Jamie to come along with me on this appointment, one of the last before the due date; I didn't want either to miss out on the details of God's promise. We checked in with the nurse and did the normal routine stuff before heading back to her office where she checked me and let me know that he was in the right position, head down, and his heart beat was good and strong. However if Paxton was stubborn and didn't make his great escape by the 14th, then I would have to be induced the day after.

Hesitant to agree because of the rocky beginning to my pregnancy, I didn't want to take the risk he wouldn't be done "baking" yet. I was scared an induction could affect him in a negative way and I didn't want anything to harm him. Jamie saw the worried look on my face and held my hand to comfort me.

At times, I was ready for him to be in the arms of Jamie and Ben but, at others, I wanted him to stay in my stomach forever. I was selfish and untrusting of God when He said Paxton would turn out fine. I had doubts because of the drugs I had done. If Paxton was in my stomach and I never saw him, than I would not have to face the baby that would expose my flaws. How could I face the child that, in the beginning, I had wanted to abort? Knowing the love I had for him now, made me feel that much more ashamed.

JAMIE

Things were coming along with the house. Ben and I had talked about the possibility of moving into something bigger as we had initially purchased our itty bitty home because we were never there except to shower and sleep and we didn't have children at the time.

Lesa and I were texting every day. We sent scriptures back and forth and talked about life. We'd meet for coffee and such to talk about the baby room and other baby things—whatever came in our mind!

Lesa had another appointment on February 8th at 11a.m. and fortunately I was able to get off to go. I met Lesa there and we headed downstairs. We went in as her name was called and did the same routine. It was just Lesa and I. The whole time I was so hopeful she would have the baby that day. As we entered the room, Lesa was told to dress down. As the curtain was closed between us, we continued to joke that she would be rushed to the hospital because Dr. Jamie would tell her she was ready.

The doctor came in and I joined Lesa at her head. I again heard the heartbeat; that never got old. She then told Lesa she was still 1 cm. dilated. He was low. Dr. Jamie joked he may not have much hair; this was the first of many times we were told he may be a baldy.

We discussed what it would look like if he didn't come Monday the 14th; she would need an induction and the only available date was the 15th. Lesa was apprehensive. From our talks, I knew she was eager to have him, get some sleep, and be comfortable but, at the same time, wanted nothing rushed.

The doctor also asked me if I had any questions. I asked what the hospital stay would look like and if I'd get to see him at all after the birth. Dr. Jamie didn't seem to know as she only worked with the pregnancy side of things. I felt kind of sheepish asking about that rather than the baby's health. I trusted the Lord with Pax's health and, at this point, the first months of his life in the womb were not even on my mind, I knew that was God's responsibility. It was another miracle; I wasn't worrying, miraculous!

Since Lesa was doing things through the local pregnancy facility, which worked with this particular OBGYN office, Jamie would not be doing the delivery but rather the O.B. Hospitalist on duty. I had been getting info from friends who worked at the hospital about the stay. The clearest info I received was that, if there was availability, we could possibly stay in the hospital but it would depend on the nurses. I would also have access and visitation privileges, like any natural mother, to the nursery. I just wanted him here, selfishly. Not just to see him and hold him, but the sooner he was born the sooner he'd be home with us, the sooner the pain and reality of taking him from her would happen and be over. I was really struggling with it. This would be what I wrestled with even after we brought him home.

I was grateful Lesa wanted an open adoption. When Ben and I first researched adoption we were completely opposed. We didn't want to have to be responsible for meetings and caring for the emotions of the birth mom. I was selfish. But the more I thought about it before I met Lesa, it just made more sense. A mother, who

wants to even just see pictures of their baby, makes me know they will take care of themselves during pregnancy because they are concerned for their baby's well-being long term.

We left the appointment and I headed to work. We kept in touch all day and I called Ben with the update. Lesa and I made plans to attend a local church's women's rally on Friday; we were stoked to hang and get spiritually refreshed. I was excited too because in a couple days we would have the last needed baby item, the car seat/stroller duo; we'd be ready!

Within weeks our home was changing, our family was expanding by two, and our faith was increasing. God had truly showed Himself faithful and true. It was undeniable God was evident in this. In every way He was providing more than enough. More than enough money, resources, support, and favor. We felt honored, extremely favored, and yet so very humble at the same time.

We were humbled under God's extraordinary love, which would consider our desire and go above our hopes to execute such an extravagant show of love. We were also humbled knowing that there would be a sacrifice from a young woman, which would bear more than pain and would break her very core as she walked in obedience to the Lord. Our favor would come from the heartache of another; we were humbled.

Rosa

On Friday morning, February 11th, I prepared myself for a busy day. I had a doctor appointment early, then an afternoon college class--which would be the first one of the semester since I began late--and then I would be meeting up with Jamie that night for a women's conference at James River Assembly. I was excited. I woke up feeling refreshed even after staying up late in anticipation of what the day held with God paving my way. With a smile on my face, as I reflected over the past several months, I headed out the door ready for the new chapter of my life.

I didn't meet anyone at this point at Dr. Jamie's. She was just doing the routine stuff, but, this time, she was going to naturally induce labor. I wasn't that afraid of this because she sounded so confident it would be fine; Paxton would be ready and if he wasn't then it wouldn't force him out. It was merely an aid to help get things started. I was however, a tad worried I would go into labor in the middle of my first day of class or at the women's rally; both seemed like a nightmare. As much as I wanted the pregnancy to come to an end so I could walk normally again, I didn't want to be the side show for people I was just making a first impression on.

I felt well after leaving the clinic and I made way to the second stop of the day--my humanities class. As Paxton was in head down position, I was having trouble bending over to pick up my backpack and books from the floor of my front seat; I could only imagine how goofy I must look to other college kids. My face was turned three shades of pink as I became increasingly embarrassed. Somehow, I pushed aside all feelings of shame and made it to class on time with everything I needed.

Sitting in the back row, I didn't want to be noticed. I looked at all the other students attending, and shuddered as they walked past me to their seats just praying they wouldn't look at me in any negative way. Hoping I wouldn't know anyone in the class, weakness buckled itself onto my knees and I knew I wouldn't be able to pay attention. Fortunately, it was the first day so we were just covering the syllabus; that meant I was able to draw pictures in my notebook of a few different cartoon babies. Glad that no one was sitting beside me, I kept the drawings to myself and internally laughed the time away.

I left class in a hurry. I had a few hours to just relax at home before the rally that night. I desperately needed a nap, but I knew if I fell asleep then I would not wake up until tomorrow. The pregnancy was starting to really take a lot out of me. Nine times out of ten, I would be found lying on the couch, feet propped in the air, and downloading music onto my computer; this was exactly what my plan was for when I arrived home.

I settled into my favorite spot and began downloading a few of my favorite Christian artists that had catchy tunes, I felt Paxton kicking away at my ribs and it made me desperately want to discipline him right then and there. Unfortunately you can't tell a baby what to do when they are in or even out of the womb this early. So I decided to play one of the songs I downloaded and sing along softly to him in hopes of soothing him.

Little did I realize my lack of telling time and

figuring out how much time is actually needed to get from point a to point b. If I was supposed to be somewhere at five, I would start getting ready and then be ready to leave by five. It was an awful habit. I sped everywhere in order not to be late and instead of seeing my car as the vehicle it is, I referred to it more as a teleportation device, one that would always let me down.

It was almost time for the women's rally and I had yet to even shower. I looked at my mismatched socks and my white sweat pants and decided I would put on a t-shirt and throw my hair up in a ponytail. Jamie would understand if I looked terrible because I was pregnant. People didn't actually expect a pregnant lady to get ready for an event, did they? As I got ready in less than ten minutes, I quickly regretted not putting on something cute, curling my hair, and being attractive. If I went into labor that night, I would be taking lots of pictures and I hated that I looked so pathetic. Oh well, all vanity aside, it was time for me to go.

JAMIE

The Lord was certainly enlarging our territory. He was giving us a baby, an heir to carry the Ward name, a child that will one day give us grandbabies. He was giving us a young woman to add to our family as well. A woman who would need our tender love and compassion, not to save her, for she was already in the Lord, but a young woman who needed the love from her Lord's bride, the church, to continue to press on in victory even after her baby was born. God was not skimping on any details either. Legalities were coming along, the home was finished, and the day before we had just gotten our car seat. Bring on the baby.

Tonight we would meet after I got off work and attend the James River Women's Rally. We both needed some Jesus refreshment and I was eager to attend a service, to worship next to her and my baby. Lesa had planned on working that weekend. The woman was crazy; she started her first set of classes today, was planning on working the weekend, and having a baby. It made me love her all the more.

During lunch, I ran to the mall to get her a necklace because the necklace I ordered had yet to come, she was due any day, and I wanted to give her something. I left work a bit early to ensure I could get decent seats at the rally. When I got to the church the sanctuary doors weren't open yet so I headed to the rally store to get a t-shirt and something for us to drink. Man I was hungry, it had been several days of fasting. I was determined this baby would be thoroughly prayed over and Lesa's delivery would be amazing. I was a bit fearful for her since she was so small she'd have a C-section. I wanted God in every part from delivery, to hospital favor, to being able to see him, to being there when he was born, to Lesa saying good bye. So I prayed specifically and blended it with fasting As soon as we were checked in to the hospital, I would get a Big Mac and extra fries!

Lesa texted she was there and was waiting in the hallway near one of the sanctuary entrances. Once I finally spotted her, I was captivated and at the same time felt so sorry for her. She looked pathetic, slumped on a bench against the wall; she would have this baby soon! I sat down next to her and gave her a hug and my gift. She was grateful for her drink and necklace and she caught me up on her first day of classes and how she was feeling.

The doors opened and we headed in. Lesa moved slowly and as we sat down we started to joke about having the baby that evening. Lesa was tired and just wanted him out. We took some pictures and worship started. I felt bad because I wanted my mind to be on Jesus but all I could think about was Paxton. I was undoubtedly thankful for the Lord's hand on it but I felt convicted my mind would only press in to thoughts of Pax.

Worship was over and we greeted people around us. Lesa had immediately sat down after worship and had to push herself up to say hello to people. Something was up. Lesa looked at me and giggled. "I think I'm having contractions." My face started to hurt from my huge smile. Now this is what I'm talking about. This was really truly happening.

We remembered what Dr. Jamie said about coming to the hospital when the contractions were 3-5 minutes apart. So we waited, timing them; Lesa giggled, then I did. She'd let me touch her belly every time. The speaker for the evening was sharing her testimony - how she got into drugs and became pregnant - how in her labor pains God was radically changing our heart. Lesa and I laughed; you have to be kidding me. Is God serious right now? The speaker continued at the very same moment her labor was happening, her pastor father was preaching and the Lord told him to stop and pray for his daughter though he had no idea she was pregnant - only lost and a runaway; the speaker then showed the audience the video of her dad's service. She then began talking about labor pains again; Lesa and I lost it!

Lesa was having contractions every 3-5 minutes and we were giggling every time it happened or at the mention of labor pains. The ladies in front of us were less than impressed, looking back at us and rolling their eyes. Finally one of them turned around as we decided to leave and asked us to be quiet because she was trying to listen. I manage a passive aggressive response," Don't worry we were just leaving, my friend here is having contractions; we're heading to the hospital and we'll be out of your way."

We head out and decide to take her car to the hospital. During contractions, Lesa had texted her mom to let her know we were headed to the hospital; she would meet us there. I texted Ben and my best friends; I drove, we laughed, Lesa labored. She didn't seem fazed. However, I had seen my mom labor; I knew we were in for a night and it was just the beginning...but I was hopeful.

Susan

February 11. Excitement! The text that Lesa is at the hospital! "Do you want me to come up?" "Sure, but only if you want to." Of course I want to! I want so much to be right there through these next hours, but do I want that just for Lesa or for myself? If there is anything I've tried to assure and reassure Lesa of these past months it's that "love is sacrificial action", our family motto--God's love for us, her love for this baby--it's so much more than a word or a feeling. I'm trying to take my own counsel because the truth is maybe the sacrifice I needed to make was not in leaving the comfort of my nice warm house to stay up all night at the hospital, but to stay put--step back and allow someone else to step in.

At different times on this journey she had asked me to be there with her on D-Day, but recently things with her mom were going smoothly... and there was Jamie now. I was absolutely praising God for both of those things, but it left me unsure of my own role. I didn't want to miss this but I didn't want to take it from anyone else either. Lesa and Paxton had been one and the same these past months, and being there for one was being there for both; the imminent separation was looming and, although I have fallen in love with this baby, my focus must remain on this young woman I have seen blossom before my eyes the past months no less dramatically than a time-lapse video of a flower from sprout to bloom.

Resa

We got to the hospital and unofficially checked in. I was still laughing when the nurse came and got Jamie and I. We headed up to one of the smaller rooms used to check me, the baby's heart, and the consistency of my contractions. The baby's heart beat was amazing. Steady and fierce. Because I was still laughing they said the contractions weren't where they needed to be. My mom, who had just arrived, heard them and quickly agreed.

The doctors told me to walk to see if anything would happen, to see if baby would move at all or my dilation would increase. So Jamie and I took off. We walked around the hospital and talked about how ironic and funny God had been and how we were so excited for the baby to be here. We couldn't wait to meet him. I wanted to see the little boy I'd been carrying. I wanted to hold him and hug him. I wanted to see his smile and hear the noises he might make!

We looked at all the newborn babies and wondered what Pax would look like. There was a baby that was like 9lbs with a perfectly round head and all the other babies had funny cone-shaped heads. We laughed more! The big baby was a C-section baby. I couldn't imagine anyone squeezing that melon out!!

After walking, we arrived back at the room. They checked me again and told me nothing was going to happen and I should go home and try to get some rest. They told me the contractions were going to stay about 2-3 minutes apart, they would get worse, and they would intensify. The pain scared me. It was going to get worse; I was supposed to try to sleep?! I didn't want to go home. What if something happened? I wanted Jamie to be there.

We left the hospital and Jamie drove me home. I started feeling my contractions beginning to get stronger. I wanted to be strong though, so I just kept a smile on my face. When we got to my house, we said our goodbyes and I told Jamie I would let her know when we were going to head back to the hospital. I watched as Jamie pulled away in my car to go to her house and it made me sad.

I wanted her to stay the night. I wanted her to experience all of what was going on. Every contraction, because if our world didn't have suffering, she would be able to get pregnant and even though the contractions were the worst part, I would want her to feel them knowing a blessing would be coming from all the pain. It was a blessing to know, I would endure this for the sake of another. God humbled me, as I lay down in my mom's room and, around 7:00 am, the strong smile on my face became pain-filled tears.

JAMie

I headed to a friend's house that Ben and I were staying with because our shower was not working. I was okay with that because it was Heather's home, we'd extended stayed before, and it was three minutes from Lesa's. If baby came, we would be there until our water was fixed which Heather loved. I thought it was pretty perfect since she's the one that told Lesa's mom about us and she's an incredible mother of four boys, she knows her stuff. I knew my baby and I would be in great hands even when Ben would have to go straight back to work after the birth.

I got to Heather's and, surprisingly, crashed next to my husband in the spare bedroom. Ben was incredibly thorough, he had packed for both of us and baby while also managing to put in our car seat. His downfall, in his hurry to get the car packed and potentially head to the hospital, was backing out of the garage with one of the back doors still opened. Poor guy, I thought it was cute, more than anything. The door stayed on but would not open.

God was undeniably good. That moment before you receive your promise is so memorable. You remember smells and sights; you're focused and feel so alive. That's the beauty of being under the lordship of a Holy Creator.

In and out of sleep, I checked my phone often and didn't hear anything. I'd drift back to sleep, only to wake up suddenly with heart palpitations with every noise that came from the house.

In the morning, Ben had left early to figure out our

water situation at the house and to get some more stuff we'd need to be comfortable at the hospital and Heather's. I finally got up, slipped out of bed, and fell on my knees. I prayed, with tears running down my face. I was thankful, emotional, grateful, and speechless.

Heather and her boys were in the kitchen getting a late start as well. They had ball games and errands to run. She and I caught up on what happened the night before and we talked about when she might go back to the hospital. I headed back to my room to make a hospital bag for myself - not knowing if Ben and I would even be able to stay, when I got the phone call. Lesa's mom had called to let us know they were heading to the hospital and she'd let me know when she was admitted.

I called Ben with the update and got ready. I was unusually slow about getting myself ready. I wanted my hair to be perfect, I wanted to look like a mother; I wanted to be put together - as if qualifying myself for the gift God was giving me. I finally was finished when I received a text she had been admitted, was dilated to 5 centimeters, and they were giving her an epidural soon.

I took Lesa's car to the hospital, stopping to fill up the tank and get Lesa's mom a soda. This was happening; everything was in slow motion. I can even remember the blue corolla in front of me the majority of my drive. Ben was at the house figuring out the water issue and wanted updates. He wouldn't answer his phone, which was unusual, but I didn't think much of it and just assumed he was busy.

Resa

No sleep...

Pain...

I cradled my stomach and curled in a ball; I tried to wait it out—tried to be tough. I didn't want to go into the hospital just to get sent home again. So I waited, as the pain increased, I thought to myself, "I don't want to waste anyone's time. I don't want to give anyone a false alarm. I have to be patient." When I couldn't take it anymore, I stood up holding my stomach with both hands, trying to keep from stumbling. I yelled for my mom. She too, had been up with me the majority of the night. It was now around noon; at this point, I had already been in the beginning stages of labor since 8pm the night before.

My mom quickly got in the car as I wobbled and stopped, wobbled and stopped my way to the passenger side door. Climbing in was a challenge. I couldn't breathe; I couldn't concentrate on anything but the pain. I slammed my feet into the floor board and kept my mouth shut as I tried to think out the pain. Saying just one minute and the pain will ease, I knew it would come back one minute later, but the minute I had between each contraction... the minute my insides didn't feel like they were being torn apart and rewired felt like heaven. I could take a breath. I could talk and think...And when my brain would begin to work...

The only thing I could manage to say in minute segments over and over was "Does Jamie know to come now? Is she on her way? Are they going to be there in time?" The drive to the hospital was the longest drive of my life. It was only thirty minutes; it seemed to be like thirty hours. I kicked and cried. I slammed my fists on the window. My mom kept telling me to breathe; I would hold my breath and the pain would last longer. I wasn't sure I could do this. It seemed that only a few minutes ago I thought contractions were funny. Now I had to humble myself and let my mom be right; they were awful.

We pulled up to the hospital, parked, and walked in. What were we thinking?! We walked all the way to the front door, got on an elevator, and walked to go check in. I was in LABOR and my knees were so weak. I just wanted the pain to go away. I was so tired.

I couldn't think of anything. I barely paid attention to what was going on around me. Before I knew it, Jamie was there and the nurses said the magic words, "You can have your epidural now!" I was hoping so bad it would work. I was scared because of all the horror stories I had heard, but the pain was unbearable. Worse than anything I had ever felt. I didn't care what they had to do. I was exhausted.

The anesthesiologist showed up moments later and asked me to scoot to the edge of the bed. Slowly, I scooted, cringing every time I had a contraction. He asked me to put my knees as close to my stomach as possible and for me to bend in a moon shape, to kind of fold in half; it seemed like mission impossible.

My mom came to my left side and held my hand as Jamie came and comforted me on my right side. The anesthesiologist asked me to bend a little more so he could put the needle in my back. It was difficult to move any further. My nerves told me that he was going to mess up.

JAMie

When I got to the hospital they let me in. I was so honored to be able to be back in the room. The nurse came in and we made sure I could be back with her during delivery; she didn't see any issue with it. I also asked about a post delivery room and they went to see if it would be possible. Lesa and I joked and laughed. She was in pain this time around - though I could still tell she was trying to keep her cool. She was silent the majority of the time. Her sister came shortly after to visit and her brother was in the room when I had arrived but was getting picked up by Lesa's dad shortly.

I left the room to call my mom; it hadn't struck me until I got there that maybe they would want to all be here. I also had had Ben call his mom in the morning to let her know the baby was possibly coming. Ben knew Lesa was admitted but I couldn't seem to reach him after that last call. I continued to call only to take a break to be with Lesa as she got her epidural.

I saw the whole thing. Lesa sat off the side of the bed, as Lesa's mom held her up on her left side and me on her right. I looked behind Lesa watching the doctor administer her epidural. I saw this tube be inserted into her back and as it stuck out there, I got a little light headed; I didn't want to be wimpy so I held the urge for a second. Still intrigued, I watched him wipe away excess ointment from her back and grab this little bag that held what looked like looped up wire. As he told Lesa he was almost finished, he stated "I'm going to string this wire into the tube and near your spine."

That's it. My stomach became undone.

I had to sit down. I apologized to Lesa - as she chuckled, I walked to the door and sat down. I was on the verge of passing out so I stuck my legs in the air, to get the blood flowing. Both Lesa and her mom laughed at me. I felt so bad, though they didn't care; I wanted to be strong for Lesa but that was intense. I should have been wise and avoided looking, like Lesa's mom.

Afterward, as any young adult after a major life event (even not-so-major events) we updated our social network status and then I went into the hall to call Ben. He was still not answering and I was panicked. All I could think was 'Great! God's giving me a baby and taking my husband; he's in a car accident, I know it."

I reached Ben's mom who was on the way and let me know she would contact Ben for me while I was with Lesa. In the middle of our call, Ben finally called back. His phone had fallen between the seat of the car and console and was on silent. He was on his way. He asked if we needed anything -- moment of truth -- I didn't hesitate. I wanted a burger, fries, and the world's largest soda! Lesa's mom was hungry too. It was the perfect time to get some food; Lesa couldn't eat and was already dozing from no sleep and the relieving effects of the epidural.

Ben arrived. We found seats in the lobby. And most importantly, at the moment, I ate...and it was good. I sat with Lesa's mom while eating and had a heart to heart. It was the first time I actually got to really talk to her. Lesa was asleep and it was a perfect time.

We had some light talk then I asked..."Are you okay, with all of this?" She looked at me surprised, but very serious. She assured me in many words she was more than okay with it. She vulnerably stated she hated that she couldn't raise another grandbaby. She and Lesa both loved us and knew this was right. A bit more comfortable, I asked, "Is Lesa sure, is she going to change her mind?" She was a little puzzled, but given the circumstances it wasn't the weirdest thing I could have said. She again assured me Lesa was sure about both of us, sure of the fact she can't raise this baby or give him the life she wants for him. The fact is, she wanted a mother and a father. She didn't doubt it would be hard but knew it was best. We continued to eat when she and Lesa's friend, Susan, arrived. I was introduced and she embraced Ben and me with such gratitude. Lesa's mom took her back to see Lesa and we stayed in the lobby.

We continually updated our statuses on our social network pages for our friends to be in the know and posted a silly video about being soon to be parents. Most of our closest friends (mostly church) were attending an event for married couples for Valentine's. We had planned to go but, of course, we had better things to do.

My parents arrived and then Ben's. We updated them on what was going on. Then, as if God himself had put His foot on the gas, it began. In the middle of me talking about how Lesa was, Lesa's mom came out to let me know she was going to begin pushing. I headed back in. All systems were a go.

Susan

I decided I'd go on up and just see how things were going, how Lesa was doing, and be a support for her and her mom; make myself available but stay on the fringe. Halfway there I got another text they were on the way back home. Good, there was still time for me to share with her how I was feeling and let her make the call.

With assurance that Lesa wanted me to be with her at the hospital, I headed on back up Saturday afternoon. I was so anxious to meet Jamie and Ben. I became excited to tell them what I believed God wanted me to share. "I know you see your prayers answered in this miracle, but remember the answer to our prayers is YOU. YOU ARE THE ANSWER!"

As I entered the room, I could see Lesa's excitement but could also sense her pain; so much deeper than the physical squeeze of the contractions was the squeeze on her heart. She tried so hard to fight both. The only thing I knew to do turned out to be a huge moment of blessing for me. I slid over to her bedside. Smoothed her hair. Stroked her eyebrows. Whispered a prayer. Whispered "I love you. I'm so proud of you. You can do this." We both knew what I meant. Not just this delivery, but this sacrifice. With sleepy, tearful eyes my girl whispered back, "Thanks for being here just for me." Thanks for letting me.

Lesa

After a decent amount of snoozing, one of the delivery nurses told me it was time to start pushing. My mom and Jamie were in the room. The nurse helped push my knees up because I couldn't feel my legs; my mom and Jamie took their positions on either side of me, just as I was taking mine. They both looked at me and grabbed each hand. I felt as though we were positioning for battle.

The delivery nurse said that since I couldn't feel my contractions, she would tell me when to start pushing. We were all so eager; for the first time she said, "Push!"

I tried to bear down and push, but with no feeling, thought my efforts were useless. I wished some of the epidural, which I had wanted so much before and now resented, would wear off so I could at least feel something! It was hard to get the hang of pushing when it didn't feel natural. After an hour of pushing and nothing to show for it, I was beginning to feel discouraged. The nurse asked me to sit and rest and we would try again soon. I looked at Jamie and my mom and told them I was scared because I didn't want to have to get a C-section.

The nurse came back and said if I couldn't push him out then a C-section would be the only option. It wasn't the scar I feared, but rather having the scar as a constant reminder that it's what I ended up with, not a baby. Surely, God wouldn't let me get a physical scar to remind me of the scar that would be on my heart. I felt motivated. I looked at Jamie and my mom and then we began again. Pushing and pushing, it just wasn't enough.

But then, I started to feel the pressure from the contractions and putting all embarrassment aside, I let Jamie and my mom hold up each leg as I pushed. I was unashamed. I pushed two times, hard; the nurse looked at me and told me to stop because the baby was coming but the doctor wasn't in the room yet. I tried to hold back but I wanted him out.

The doctor seemed to take forever, but as soon as he got in the room, I gave two more hard pushes and with some encouragement from Jamie and my Mom announcing each time his head was out and then his shoulders and to give one last push....He was out.

While the doctor held crying Paxton, Jamie was asked to cut the umbilical cord. Her face was flushed in excitement. She grabbed the scissors so shakily because of her overflowing joy and after two squeezes on the scissors, Paxton was free from me and then the doctor's assistant attempted to hand him back to me.

Then, the hardest words that have ever escaped my mouth were spoken into existence. "No, give him to his mother."

My heart was broken. I wanted to be the first one to hold him so bad, but then I saw him placed in her arms. And she began to love him, with all the mess; I watched as she kissed him and began crying. Her tears were contagious; my mouth was smiling but my eyes were crying, portraying the outside appearance of my afflicted flesh and spirit... And I saw Gods promise fulfilled in her eyes.

They then took little Paxton to be cleaned; Jamie and my mom followed. I was stuck where I was. I had yet to see his face. I was being stitched up and even though my mom stayed by my side, I felt as if everyone had forgotten about me. They all huddled around the baby, and I was left broken in pieces in the hospital bed. I could hear them all oohing and awwwing behind nurses in my view; all I wanted to do was stand up and be with Paxton and the rest of them.

I had been living for Paxton the past nine months, doing things that I would want him to be proud of. So when he was placed in Jamie's arms, I felt as if I was giving up my life, and placing it in her arms also.

I gave birth to new life and that life gave birth to a new feeling I had never experienced: love, in the purest, most sacrificial, form… true selfless love.

I then asked the doctors to do something for me before they left the room; I wanted Ben to experience this moment since he couldn't share in the exact second when his wife gave birth. I asked Jamie to let him in to see his son. She ran to the door and Ben and my sister came into the room. Paxton was placed in Bens arms for the first time. I could feel The Holy Spirit; I could feel the love that surrounded us and, in my brokenness, I found peace.

JaMie

We had been there during a few shift changes so the doctor delivering was changing, as well as the nurses. The doctor delivering was the very doctor I had prayed would. He had incredible report and I so badly wanted him included in this. My heart was at rest, I knew we were in great hands.

Finally, the nurses were changing and Lesa was told in all seriousness the baby has been low for a while and needed to be out. He would have some serious crowning; if she couldn't push him out the next round, she'd need a C-section.

She was determined to get him out. I was hopeful she would too, as I would not be able to see him if she was operated on. So we relaxed for a few; time dragged on. Then the nurses came. The nurse we had when Lesa checked in the night before was back. This was a relief because she knew our history and we knew that she was cool with me being there. We talked a bit; then Lesa was told to push. Her epidural was wearing off perfectly. She wasn't feeling the pain but knew when the contractions were coming. She was bearing down incredibly. Between pushes, the nurse promptly asked her to stop; the baby was coming. It seemed Lesa was determined after all. Lesa informed her that the doctor needed to get in here because she needed to push. As if the request was completely not doable. The doctor was delivering two other babies at the same time, so emotions were all over the place.

The room filled with people. They were making things happen like nobody's business. I was witnessing a birth and it was incredible. The doctor entered and

Lesa pushed. Within minutes, what was seemingly a bit gross, yet intriguing to me, became a supernatural, undeniable, favorable moment.

At 7:58pm, my son was born. The doctor's assistant went to hand the baby boy to Lesa when she stopped her and introduced me as his mother. She turned away slightly as to keep from accepting what was undeniably hers, so I could receive what God had taken from her to give to me. I lost it. I had never had that kind of selfless introduction in my life. As soon as I knew it, I held my son.

Tears.

I kissed him ever so lightly. Lesa's mother dropped her daughter's hand to grab my camera without any thought to capture my first moment with my son. I didn't even ask. I was undone; they were so selfless. They truly blessed me. I will never ever forget that, ever.

Ben

After waiting in the hallway for what seemed like days, with my face pressed to the floor so my ears could at least capture the sound of my first child's birth, he came. When I walked in, Lesa, the birth mother of my child, asked me without hesitation one of the best questions I'd ever been asked - If I would like to hold my son.

There he was; all 7 pounds, 5 ounces and 21 inches long, right in front of me, swaddled in a blanket in the arms of a woman that I could never repay. The emotion inside of me was like none that I had ever felt. It was greater than joy, greater than happiness, greater than excitement, greater than love. The emotion was unexplainable.

Let me tell you a little bit about myself. I have wanted to be a father since the day I got married. I LOVE kids. Ask anyone. I am drawn to them and for some reason they are drawn to me. I told Jamie as soon as she was ready we were going to do it (pun intended). Every fiber in me was ready to be a father. I know I am created for many reasons and one of them, most assuredly, is to be a father. A father to children birthed by my wife or through adoption. So, after close to four years of unsuccessful attempts at becoming a father, there I was, a little after 8pm on February 12 finally seeing my miracle alive; my promise fulfilled!

Lesa's sister was there; she and I lay on the floor with our ears pressed against the door as much as possible to hear what was happening in that room. I remember hearing the nurses say "okay stop pushing we have to get the doctor" because the baby was

coming. I remember hearing the doctor enter. I remember hearing laughter. I remember hearing the word push a few times. I remember hearing silence. And then, my most memorable moment of that night, I heard my baby boy cry for the very first time.

Since I couldn't go into the room I ran out to the waiting rooms and informed everyone there that Pax was here. I seemed to have overheard the measurement wrong and told everyone he was 31" long, I didn't know any better. I was hugging family and friends until Jamie came and said I could come into the room.

There he was, my promise! Lesa handed him to me. This woman gave me a miracle, just placed in my arms a beautiful, breathing miracle. She trusted me to be his father; I was honored.

JAMIE

I took him over to finish being cleaned and weighed. He weighed 7 pounds, 5 ounces and was 21 inches long. Pictures were sent to Ben and the family waiting in the lobby. Once I was cleared to open the door, I went out to tell Ben. We embraced and looked at each other in disbelief. Hand in hand we walked out to the lobby to personally announce our son's birth. In all the excitement, I hadn't realized he had already announced Paxs birth. When we came out, we found some of our friends had arrived and more were coming. After we updated them I was eager for Ben to hold Pax.

As I entered, Lesa was holding him. I won't forget it. Ben came in and went straight for Lesa. He kissed her forehead and looked at her. And before setting his eyes on his son, he asked if she was okay. That was my husband, a true gentleman. Lesa, chuckled, I think she was a bit taken back that Ben would be concerned with her. She then made the honorable gesture; she asked Ben if he would like to hold his son. It was perfect; Ben embraced his son. For the first time it became real to Ben; he was a dad.

We talked with Lesa for a bit and then Pax had to be taken to the nursery to be given his first bath. I knew the nurse's aide taking him to the nursery; she was incredible and allowed us to stop in the lobby for all our family to see. Heather and her husband were there too. Our parents couldn't get enough pictures.

It was all happening so fast.

The nurse's aide let me know they'd be prompt and also told us the most wonderful news (as if it could get any better). They had a room for us! It would be right next to Lesa's room at the end of the hallway near the nursery. We could stay until Pax was discharged!

Ben and I followed our baby to the nursery and then took the long way back to get to our rooms. We held hands and couldn't say much except that he was a daddy, I was a mommy, and we had a baby.

As we got to our room we had some visitors, plus our family, all waiting till Pax would return. While I was waiting, I decided to go see Lesa one last time in the delivery room as they still hadn't moved her. Her friend had brought her a drink and I brought her my gratitude. I just loved her more than I ever thought! She was exhausted and soon to be moved to her room to rest. I gave her a hug and we talked briefly about what the first night entailed. We could have the baby in our room to feed and bond with, while she got much needed rest. She had just birthed a baby she had carried for months and was now allowing me to nourish and bond with him his first night of life outside of her.

I couldn't believe her selflessness. I left, walking down the hall alone; I fell to the floor in an abandoned hallway, like a baby I bawled. God was in that place. I could feel Him. He had given me a healthy baby boy and an incredible woman to show me raw humility.

I headed back to our room. We had even more visitors. After an hour and a half, Pax was brought to our room. We were given bracelets as if we were the natural parents. I had a mommy band and I was crying. Most of our visitors had left, as it was getting late. But those who were there got the privilege of meeting our son, including most importantly, my apprehensive parents.

Immediately, my parents were hooked. My most

cherished moment was when my dad held him, his first grandchild. He was undone. It was so tender to see him love my son, embrace him and not want to let him go.

As the last few left, with my mom, younger sister and few best girlfriends still there - I stripped myself and him down and I fed him his bottle skin to skin. It was perfect; he was perfect. God was SO PERFECT! After the feeding we had some more guests and they got their fill. My parents decided to stay in town and help with the house the next day. All I could find myself saying was God was so good.

We said good night to our last visitors. And then there were three. We sent Pax to the nursery for a few hours to get checked up. We preferred him with us, but since he was a BUFA BABY (Baby Up For Adoption) he had to have lots of tests ran on him. At 3:00 A.M., Pax visited again for some skin on skin and a bottle. He returned to the nursery for more vitals and returned again about 6:30 for another bottle and remained on my chest until about 8:00. Then he was whisked away to meet his pediatrician in the nursery.

I crashed again and awoke at 9:30 to our baby entering Lesa's room; my heart sank. I didn't want her to change her mind. I mean, the baby was perfect; I was in love. We were in love. The next few days would be hard and my heart couldn't handle the wall between him and me.

Either way I had made up my mind; I was going to be loving, tender, patient and, as Lesa as my mentor, I was going to be selfless. I loved Lesa and we were grateful. So, in my gratitude, I gave her the only gift that truly meant something and really the only gift I

could give (that in reality wasn't really mine to give), space; space and time with her child. Receiving our promise was going to cost. As believers, we received a promise because God sent his Son to die for us and qualify us for God's goodness. He doesn't promise no pain or heart ache; He does promise to be faithful. So we had to hold on to the fact that God is faithful!

Although we were in our own separate rooms, I felt anything but separate from the Ward family. The relationship we developed over the last few weeks had proven stronger than some of those I had made over the last few years. I loved the Wards and their compassion continued to convict me to carry out this sacrificial obedience to God. As much as I would want to give Paxton up easily, it was God that truly kept my attitude willing.

My heart yearned to hold Paxton, to admire every inch of his body, to engrave it in my mind so when he left with them, he wouldn't completely be gone from me. I waited to hold his tiny fingers, to kiss his tiny nose, to tickle his tiny feet that felt much more tiny than when he had been kicking me; the anticipation was unbearable.

I had never heard any mothers talk about how bad the after effects of pregnancy are. I have heard the pain of child birth but, to me, sitting here in the hospital bed right after giving birth was much, much worse. I ached with pain regardless of the medication. Maybe this part was never talked about because the adrenaline of holding a new born baby took away all pain. However, that was not how my situation played out.

In a hospital bed, I awaited a baby, a baby born to me, a baby I never expected in a million years, and a baby that needed more than I could give. Negativity set in and it was anything but a stranger. What if Paxton had opened his eyes and saw Jamie first, then he would call her mother and not recognize me. I know this isn't a "bird" scenario, but I couldn't help thinking about the attachment we had only days before and now it seemed unreal. What if he didn't like me? What if he knows I won't be around? What if he thinks I abandoned him?

Questions that seemed logical to me were pushed out when Jamie poked her head in the room. After the brief moment of skepticism, I sought comfort from the one that orchestrated the entire circumstance. I began to relax. I appreciated that Jamie had come in a few times to see how I was doing and if I needed anything. Her concern and devoted kindness kept me from looking down at the ground for too long and rather at the situation for what it really was, a miracle.

Nurses continued to make their way in and out of my room as well. I received quite a bit of medication, and then a nurse came in with some paperwork for me to fill out. I felt so out of it. I filled it out the best I could, praying I was signing my name correctly as my hand was shaking. Then another nurse came in with the birth certificate.

"If I write his name how I like it, does it matter since it's getting changed anyway?"

"No," she replied, "If he's being adopted it doesn't matter what you put down, we just need it for our records."

For a brief moment, my mind raced back to Chase...wishing he could be here to experience this love. I wanted to honor him so I wrote down the name we had picked out together, Charlie Paxton Oliver Ward. It just seemed right at the time. Because of my inability to let go of my past I caused a problem for my future. (It's one thing to change a last name on legal papers, but another to change a first. Little did I know this would cause a speed bump in the adoption process and all the paperwork would have to be redone)

Before I knew it, I awoke to squeaking of little wheels, Paxton was pushed into my room. I wanted to stand up and bolt over to him, scoop him up and embrace him. The nurse picked him up and placed him in my arms. For the first time, I was getting to hold the little baby that had been my inspiration. I gratefully snuggled him and kissed his forehead, his mouth, all his fingers and all his toes, the pain vanished; I felt the inseparable bond between a mother and her son.

Visitors came and went from my room. I enjoyed the company, but at the same time all I wanted to do was hold Pax to myself...to not let anyone hold him because I would feel robbed of my time with him...but I was conflicted. I wanted people to share in the moment and love him as much as I did, but I didn't want to let go of him. I kept placing him in the arms of family and friends and watched as they smiled.

The day came to a close and everyone had held Paxton a few times, all had held Paxton with loving adoration. My mom was with me and I was thankful she hadn't left my side. She had been so helpful and comforting. Although I wanted alone time with Pax, I was scared to be on my own with him. I am not sure why fear crept in when all I wanted to do was kiss him and fall asleep with him in my arms. The nurse that was rounding up the night came in and gave me my last few pills. She left and as soon as she did my eyes got heavy. I didn't want to fall asleep. I didn't want to sleep away my time with Pax, but I had to swallow my fears. I lay Paxton close to my body, tucked sweetly in my arms, closed my eyes, and simply drifted off.

JaMie

Our son was born, yet he had two mothers. The reality of adoption had become real.

I was unsure how Lesa was doing and was told by the nurse she was resting. Paxton was born at 7:58 P.M. and was brought to our room throughout the night and early morning to be fed. He had many visitors from our church family and one of my girlfriends that worked at the hospital stopped to see the little miracle. The next morning, Paxton's first morning was going to be with Lesa, until then (minus his vitals in the nursery) Ben and I were going to have him.

I did not carry him in my womb but he was undeniably mine. My love for him was unreal. The fear we wouldn't connect vanished the very moment I held him and kissed his little head. He was my son given from the Lord.

At nine in the morning he was taken to Lesa. As I heard the crib being wheeled into her room and not mine my heart sank. I was devastated; I had spent the whole night with him and was in love. His attachment to me was supernatural. God's presence was in our room. I felt the empty piece filled to overflowing. Now she would have him for the next few days as we agreed and wanted, for her.

But I feared. I feared he was going to forget me and be drawn to her; the one who loved him and nourished him for months, the one who was familiar. I feared more. She carried him for nine months, she would fall even more in love, and she would change her mind.

The whole night we had him, it was as if all my

worries and fears, now that he was here, had arrived. I kept telling Ben faithlessly, "she will change her mind. You saw him, he's perfect; she isn't going to want to give him to us." Ben was tender and comforting. We were at our most humble and undeniably broken.

I kept thinking I must have felt like Abraham. He received his heir, Isaac, finally after years. And then God asked him to sacrifice him. I had to remember the Word said, "Early the next morning, Abraham set out..."-Genesis 22:3. He was prompt and complete in his obedience. He bound his son, the one he loved, and prepared to kill him to honor God's request. But in Abraham's full obedience, right before he strikes Isaac, God stops him. By Abraham's obedience, God was honored. God honored Abraham's faith with a ram. God gave Abraham something else to sacrifice.

He goes on to say in verse 17 and 18, "This is what the Lord says: Because you have obeyed me and have not withheld even your son, your only son, I swear by my own name that I will certainly bless you. I will multiply your descendants beyond number, like the stars in the sky and the sand on the seashore. Your descendants will conquer the cities of their enemies. And through your descendants all the nations of the earth will be blessed--all because you have obeyed me."

I wanted to honor God. He was my reward, not Pax. I realigned my focus, my faith, and I put my trust in the Almighty. We were able to see him a bit the next few days and had family visit. My parents were in love with Pax. Ben's close relatives that lived in town visited and got to meet him briefly. We did not want to over step and take Lesa's time with him. I was able to spend time with Lesa. I just wanted to hang out with her - but I didn't want her to think I was coming to just oversee her time with Pax. I genuinely wanted to see her. We also got our online gift in the mail - a necklace with a brass shoe and a blue pearl and a "C" for Charlie engraved on a small medallion. Lesa had set her mind and connection with him as baby Charlie.

As much as I wanted to see her and make sure she was okay, I wanted to hold and be with Pax more. It was different now. The Promise had come. It was no longer about Lesa or us; it was about him.

I just remember I never left the hospital. I didn't want to miss any chance to see Pax or any news of him and his 'check-ups'. The first morning the pediatrician we picked got to see him and was so incredible with our needs, as soon to be full-time parents. He let us know Pax was healthy and really strong. He actually lifted his head up the first morning of life while on his belly when getting checked. We were so proud. At the same time we were so nervous and emotional. I would find myself crying, in gratefulness but also in waves of fear and impatience. I just wanted to bond with him. I also cried at the thought of what I was doing; I was taking a baby from a woman.

More than all the details of the next few days, what I remember most was the spiritual heaviness that was happening. I KNEW Pax was God's gift to us. I had to remain faithful Lesa would stay obedient in giving us Paxton. The first night in the hospital there was some serious spiritual stuff going on. Ben and I could feel it. As much as I felt the Lord's presence - we both felt a battle. We knew God had something huge in store for this little baby. Ben and I didn't doubt it, nor do I think the enemy was oblivious to it.

The next day I woke to find Paxton was being wheeled into my room in his little cart. My mom had been up for a while and the nurses had brought me breakfast. I was extremely hungry and ready to chow down, but I wanted to hold Paxton and relish this last day with him. New flowers had made their way onto my window sill and a stack of cards sat beside the hospital bed. It was encouraging to know so many people were behind me and supported me. I could feel everyone's love; I was thrilled to tell everyone about the miracles Jesus was performing in my life and people's lives around me.

Throughout the day, more visitors stopped in and got their pictures taken with little Pax. We had a ball just talking about how tiny he was, how he did have a little hair, since no one believed he would, and how cone-shaped his head was. I put a small hat on his head to keep everyone from making fun of him but, as soon as I took it off, I styled what little hair he had into a very stylish Mohawk. He just looked so precious.

I changed him about 3 times into little outfits I selected for him and watched as he turned bright red when he didn't like it. Even his cry was adorable. I, selfishly, slowly changed him and admired every attribute and little detail. Then I swaddled him back up and watched as he calmed down. His personality made me fall in love with him even more, if that's possible.

The day ended rather quickly, the sun lowered in the sky and my mom let out a large yawn. She had been with me for two days and I knew that she was exhausted. I wanted her here with me, but I knew she needed to rest in her own bed. Tomorrow was going to be a hard day; she was going to need strength for both of us.

"Go home Mom, you're tired and I will be fine. It's just me and Pax; I don't mind hanging out with him on my own." The second part of my statement was true, but I was nervous to not have her there.

She reluctantly agreed knowing she needed to get some good sleep after just having a small recliner to sleep on the night before. She left and I immediately called Susan. She was close by and I knew that she would stay with me for a little while. When she got to the room, my mom had already gone and she looked surprised. "Don't worry, I sent her home." I told her as I watched her face go from confused to relieved.

Susan sat right next to me, tickling little Paxton's feet as I held him. I wanted her to provide me with comfort and be by my side, but I also wanted to keep Paxton all to myself. I didn't want her holding him. As I watched her gleam at baby Pax and continually care for me, I put aside all selfishness and handed her Pax. I was sleepy, but this was my last night with him, so I willed myself to stay up no matter what it would take. I would fight for the time I would get to spend with him.

A few hours later, Susan said her good-byes. Concerned, she looked at me and said, "Are you sure you're going to be okay by yourself? I can stay if you need me to. I don't mind." A smile stretched across my face. I loved that she was so compassionate. I loved her heart was so willing, that she would sleep on a rock hard chair just to make sure I was okay. "No, it's fine. I sent my mom home too. I understand that you both need your sleep and besides, it will be fun to just have some Paxton and I time. I haven't been alone with him yet." I insisted.

I was finally alone, alone with Pax. I picked him up and lay him down in my arms. I put him in the middle of my legs, knees bent so his face would be looking directly into mine, and I held his hands. I stared at him, mesmerized. I grabbed my phone and began taking pictures with him. Every move he made I wanted to document. Every hand motion, every sleeping face, and every leg kick I wanted frozen in time.

I picked him up again, rested his little head on my shoulder, and held him tight. In this moment alone with him, just listening to him breathe and his little baby coos as he slept...I began to cry. Softly, I sang to him through tears, in prayer and in praise, I asked God to watch over him and asked Paxton not to forget me if I didn't get to see him often. This was out of my hands and in God's; as much as I wanted to have faith, I had doubt.

A rocking chair looked at me from the corner of the room. Still holding Paxton tightly to my shoulder, we made our way to the rocking chair. As we sat and rocked, a feeling began to fill the room; not any ordinary feeling. It was uneasy, unhappy and fearful. Paxton then squirmed as I sat him on my lap and he looked up at me wide eyed. He was looking so much deeper into my eyes than I had ever experienced; it was as if he was looking so deep he ended up looking past me. A noise from behind the curtain that hid the bathroom made me jump.

Was this the medication? Was I going crazy? Why was I so scared? Why was the silence so loud? What were the voices filling this room? Was I ruining the

one night I would have alone with Paxton? I shakily grabbed the curtains and slung them back. Nothing was there. I was losing it. I couldn't shake the feeling of being threatened. Scared, I crawled back into the bed and tried to play a little music. I turned the lights on bright and cradled Pax. I needed Jamie… the presence... whatever it was...wasn't leaving and I couldn't fight it. I felt so exposed and unprotected. Then a knock at the door sat me straight up and I became wide eyed just like Paxton had been moments before.

JAMie

I believe in demons. I believe in the Devil. I believe he doesn't desire goodness or for us to have hope. He is a liar and a cheat. Jesus came to set things straight. He died for us to have POWER over everything the enemy throws our way. Jesus went as radical as death because of the reality of spiritual warfare.

I say all that to share and document the next few paragraphs.

Ben and I were spurred to pray many times throughout the day. For Paxton, for Lesa, for the adoption but also for Paxton's life - what God was calling him to do. We sought God on direction, guidance and wisdom on how to raise him up. A battle was ragomg and all we could do was pray. As we waited, while Lesa got her time with him, we prepared ourselves in prayer. And we weren't off from our senses. A very real battle happened.

The second night in the hospital, the plans were made, baby Paxton would stay with Lesa. I was broken; I yearned for him. She would have visitors; they would hold my baby, share in his first days of life and we didn't know them. We would hear him cry and I would weep. Ben would hold me close and we'd snuggle on the hospital bed in our room. We were able to give Paxton good night kisses, tell Lesa sweet dreams, and go into our room, shut the door and snuggle on the bed really intended for one. We eventually fell asleep. We were restless; I was waking up often, sweating, crying, and praying. Something wasn't right. I fell back asleep only to be woken up by Ben saying,

"Jamie, Jamie...go check on Lesa and Pax. Go into her room."

He was serious. This was real. This was urgent. We could feel it. There was something spiritually happening in her room.

I knocked on her door and peeked in with her "come in". She was on her bed, sitting erect and alert. She looked exhausted and was holding Pax closely. Something was in her room. I knew she hadn't slept since the night before. By her very appearance, she was very much aware of what I was feeling. But I didn't know where she stood with the reality of spiritual warfare and such. At this moment, it became clear to me why the Lord had called me to fast. I mumbled prayers under my breath as I sat down in her rocker. It was warm; she had been here recently. I peered at her and we talked for a moment. She began to relax. She showed me pictures of herself and Pax while messing with her computer. I prayed lightly. Whatever was in here was moving. I rebuked it, and then the room got silent; even though it sort of was. Pax was asleep, Lesa on her computer and phone, and I on the rocker. I can't explain it but it was loud, uneasy and "busy", then it all went away.

I looked at Lesa as she was blasting worship music from her gadget. She set her computer up near the sink and continued to hold Pax. I asked her if she needed anything. She just wanted me to stay; so I stayed. She relaxed in her bed and laid her head back. Still holding Pax she asked me how we were. I began to tell her when she dozed off. I kind of giggled because it was instant. I said "Lesa" a few times loudly as I got up and walked towards the bed; then, making sure Pax was okay, I prayed. I touched her hand and shoulder and prayed. Out loud, I prayed. I sat back down and just watched them sleep. A few moments later Pax began to cry. I waited to see if Lesa would wake up. She never moved as he began to cry harder. She obviously was exhausted. So I took Pax from her chest and changed him. I was unsure when he had last eaten but, from his serious sucking gestures, I made the decision to feed him. Lesa woke up when the nurse came to check on her. We chatted a moment and she dozed back to sleep. I stayed in the rocker just holding him. It was the first time I was able to have a moment alone with him without visitors since our first night.

It was about five in the morning at this time and my best friend, April, was working in the hospital. I walked Pax to our room and April was able to snuggle him a bit. I left Lesa and my door open in hopes that if I heard her wake up I could bring him back in. I felt guilty having him in our room so at about 6 or 7 I put him back with her and headed to the cafeteria with April to eat. I had the worst migraine and hadn't left the maternity floor since Pax's birth but I needed to get away and just process. April was timely and in this moment I was reminded why I loved her so much. She didn't do anything extraordinary; she merely stayed with me and talked. She rubbed my back and fed me pain medicine. I was an emotional basket case; she was unfazed, encouraging, and nurturing.

I headed back to the room. The day had started. I needed a nap; so I napped in hopes when I woke we would be given our discharge papers.

Resa

The morning came too soon. I was still tired and achy, as well as uncertain, but willing to carry out the plan God had so ingeniously devised. I shifted around in my bed and mentally prepared myself. I couldn't believe how surreal everything had become. My mom was sitting next to my bed and Pax was soon brought to our room. I walked over and picked him up. I had a little outfit for him, but Jamie had the cutest "Hello Ladies" outfit for him which was quite appropriate because it was Valentine's Day! So I asked her if he could wear it. She came in and changed him into it. He was so precious, so delicate.

After Jamie left the room, about an hour later Ben came in with roses for me. They were beautiful. It helped keep me strong in knowing they loved Pax; their show of love for me made it easier to come to a place of peace.

As I cuddled his face, while wiping the few tears I had, my mom and I chatted and shared in the bitter-sweet, glorious moment of relinquishing all doubts and ultimately placing Paxton into the arms of another family. I took more photos of Pax and talked to him. I gave him all the hugs and kisses I could give him before he became surrendered unto God's perfect will. I kept staring at the clock, praying for just a little more time, just a few more minutes, seconds even. To hold "the treasure" God had unburied in my heart, exposing it for me to see but not to have.

Time passed and the time for Paxton to go became mere minutes away. Jamie came in and sat next to me.

She put on his little Sock Monkey hat. She held his hand as I held him and pain held my heart. Jamie let me know his car seat was ready and walked out of the room to give me my last moments with Paxton. My mom and I cradled him and shared in a group hug. We then began to walk him to Ben and Jamie's room. I was given the honor of placing him in his car seat.

As we entered their room, they stepped out so we could place him in his car seat and say our goodbyes. I held Paxton's tiny fingers and kissed every inch of his face while buckling him in. It was at this moment my mom began to cry. After trying to hold it together, tears began to trickle from my eyes. I closed my eyes to keep them from coming out; I wanted to be strong. I wanted my mom, Ben, and Jamie to know everything was going to be okay. Unfortunately, like a dam that can't hold back water anymore, tears came bursting out from behind my closed eyelids.

Undeniably, I began thinking of how my tears were showing my failure. How could I comfort my mother when I am crying? How am I going to let Paxton see me crying? This isn't sad; this is a wonderful blessing God has chosen me for!! Get it together. Be strong!

I started to feel anger grab me, and then I saw the wheel chair being rolled up the hallway. After one last picture, I pried my hand away from his little fingers and walked into the hallway to give Ben and Jamie hugs and blessings. I want to just run out; I didn't want to look pitiful and sit in a wheelchair to be rolled out. I wanted to cry but didn't want anyone to see me. So I was mad at myself for being such a baby and mad that people were surrounding me so I couldn't let myself cry. I heavily sat myself down into the wheelchair, flowers in hand. The nurse started to wheel me away; I couldn't bring myself to look back, I couldn't stop staring forward as if to suggest to everyone I was strong and could move on.

As we were wheeling down the hallway, I saw this lady in a wheelchair. Unlike me she was holding her baby, her tightly swaddled baby. She was glowing and smiling. Her husband was behind her; he had the same glow on his face. He leaned down to kiss her as we wheeled past them. I looked down at my flowers, and wished more than anything for them to turn into a baby.

Still trying to hold it together, I remained silent. My mom had gone to get the car and I was alone with the nurse that had been pushing me. She was silent for the elevator ride, and I didn't mind. I didn't want to fill the silence. I felt as if everything I loved had just been taken and as the emotion of heartbreak was standing still, so were the sounds of my surroundings; I wanted to keep it that way. I knew as soon as my mouth opened, my heart would release all the thorns in tears and yelling.

When we got off the elevator, I was wheeled to the front door of the hospital; it was there my wish was compromised when the nurse began to speak to me. She told me she admired me for what I had done; she thought I was strong and courageous. She said she could never do that. Instead of saying anything, I just thought "yeah, I could never do it either, but I did". I stared down and looked at my toes, then my eyes averted to my tummy that, unexpectedly, was relatively the same size it was when I was carrying Paxton; it was now hollow and empty visually resembling how I felt inside.

As I sat impatiently waiting for my mom to bring the car, the testing of my faith was not over. Jamie had come down, and stood right next to me. She put Paxton's car seat right...next... to... me. I had said my goodbye already and seeing him again, in this moment, crushed me. I was so happy to see him again, but I wanted to reach down and pick him up and never let him go. I tried again to be strong and not let her see me upset or sad. I said goodbye to Jamie as my mom pulled up and the nurse wheeled me out. I couldn't bring myself to say goodbye to Paxton again.

As I pulled myself into the car, I said goodbye to the nurse that had showered me with kind words, looked at my mom that had already put on her sunglasses, shut the door, and then automatically sank into my seat. I was hurting and angry. I felt so cold inside and to make it worse the sun was shining, making me mad at God. To myself, I began to ask God why He would allow the sun to shine on such a sad day. I felt as though God was happy and it wasn't fair He would be happy when He knew I was hurting.

Jamie

After an eventful early morning, I awoke at 11:00
A.M. after falling asleep a few hours earlier because of
a migraine. It was either the lack of sleep or stress that
had brought it on. I was a million emotions which
quickly became one when my husband entered the
room with roses. It was Valentine's Day. Pax's original
due date was today and we were taking him home.

I was even more proud of Ben because he was
coming from Lesa's room after giving her flowers. He
was going to be a great provider, an incredible father. I
knew he loved Lesa and this was the only way he was
comfortable to tell her. He was grateful, he was in love
with her child, and he was humbled. I took some time
alone, locking myself in our hospital bathroom doing a
devotion and praying. I wept in my shower, pathetic
and broken. I was going to be taking a baby home,
while the woman we had fallen in love with went home
empty handed.

The day couldn't go by fast enough. We met with
our pediatrician; he let us know Pax was healthy and
ready to go home. All of our hopes (including Lesa's)
were he would be discharged before Lesa. But as the
day dragged on with no bonding time with Pax (I
realize this sounds selfish but being honest) and with
the constant feeling if we did get time it would take
away from hers, we cuddled on the bed. I would weep
in frustration and conviction. With every new hour
came a new nurse who had no idea what was going on
and needed to be updated on our 'circumstance' only
delaying the 'release.' Discharges in themselves take

seemingly forever, and then tack on legal logistics.

We finally received answers at about 3:00 P.M. We met with the lawyer we provided for Lesa and with the hospital social worker. After many questions and statements, Lesa's lawyer suggested we cover certain costs we hadn't originally agreed on. We were willing to do this, especially after we had already created a bond with Pax; there was not much we wouldn't do. The hospital social worker took our identifications, only to question mine which showed a blonde and I was currently a red head. She had to leave and 'run it through' with Lesa. Honestly I was annoyed, my profession as a hair stylist was coming between us and the swift release of our son.

Lesa and her mom were getting in their time with Paxton. At this point, no one knew we would see each other so much; all we knew was it was going to be about twice a year, so I was trying to be respectful. They were making trips back and forth to the nursery to get his feet and hand prints. My body ached. I couldn't take her baby away while, at the same time, I couldn't wait to get my hands all over him. I couldn't wait to lay him down in our bed and snuggle as a family. But she was so happy holding him and walking back and forth past our door with him.

I felt like the hospital was making it worse and dragging it out. Then finally, about 4:45 I entered Lesa's room to say goodbye. We were free to leave. I wanted to honor her time with him but it was time for him to come home. I realize the rest of what I type may seem heartless, that's not my intent. Lesa knows the Lord directed her to this decision; I knew I had supernaturally birthed Pax from my heart. He was ours;

I was his mother and Ben was his father. Lesa meant more to me than any other person on the whole planet. Her faith and obedience were a daily conviction to me. I'm a mother because of her sacrifice.

With the news, Lesa took more pictures with Pax and handed us copies of his foot and hand prints. As her nurse came in with papers it seemed Lesa was now also being released. We all dreaded this. We had asked all the nurses that we be released way before her. Now we were leaving together, making good byes impossible. Lesa eventually made it to our room as Ben was finishing loading the car. She kissed Paxton and laid him in his car seat sitting on our bed. She began to strap him in when he started to cry. She couldn't handle leaving him with his last moments being ones of tears. I stepped in, with the prompting of Ben's nudge, and began to help her strap him in. My heart sank and my body went cold. We hugged. We said good byes to let Lesa and her mom have some last moments with Pax. As we were headed out the door, Lesa's nurse showed up at our door with her wheelchair.

Don't get me wrong, I was mega grateful to have been so well taken care of at the hospital, later finding out our stay was free. But the complexity of so many shift changes and some nurses unwilling to understand what was going on was frustrating.

Lesa was taken down before us (against all our requests); we stalled to give her time to catch an elevator to the first floor and get their car. However, as we left the hospital, we ran into her again in the main lobby. She was in her wheel chair waiting for her mother to pull up. She held only the flowers Ben had given her that morning. Our stomachs fell to the floor and both our hearts broke. We were walking out with a diaper bag, flowers, and a baby in a brand new car seat.

We stopped to say one last good bye, but Lesa was distant. She was still sweet, but it was as if she had already begun preparing her heart to separate from him, for a time, with every foot of distance she took from him. Her mother pulled up seconds later. Ben had gone to get the car while Lesa, her nurse, Pax and I waited. I watched her get loaded in her car. She seemed limp and lifeless; she gave only a bleak smile at us before shutting the door. Ben pulled up right as she pulled away.

Lesa

The car ride felt so long; I just wanted to be home. I wanted to hide from the world; I wanted to let my guard down. I wanted to just give it to God, but couldn't stop my heart from hurting. When we pulled into the driveway, after a long silent car ride, my mom and I both got out of the car. My body felt so heavy; I walked slowly, dragging myself into the house. It was even difficult to open the door. I left it open so my mom could come in. I was becoming so weak; my legs shuffled along the carpet toward my bedroom. Was I dreaming? Why didn't I have control of my body? I made it to my room just in time.

My knees gave out and I found myself falling into my bed, collapsing in my grief. Like a volcano, deep, gasping sobs erupted from my core. I let go; breaking down, giving up. My mom came in and broke down with me, our broken hearts on display to each other. She held me as I uncontrollably wept. Together, we pushed through the suffering.

After lying in bed all day, I felt as if I would be in distress forever. However, through my tears I knew what I had to do. Painfully, I completely surrendered the hole in my heart, which Paxton had been filling, to God. In no time, God reached down His comforting hand and, as He picked me up in my brokenness, I began to heal.

Debbie

When Pax was born I felt disconnected, like I wasn't purposed to be his grandmother. Normally, like with my other daughter, I would have had the nurturing love wanting to squish their child with all kinds of kisses but, most important in this moment, was for his adoptive mom to experience the first moments with him. I was afraid of getting to close and feeling anything. To be honest, I didn't want it to hurt when he didn't come home with us.

I kept my distance for the next few days. I visited whenever I could, but wanted Lesa to spend time with her baby before she had to give him up. I, of course, was scheduled all weekend at work. I stopped by after work on Sunday night. I knew the next day was going to be tough. Lesa would be going home; Jamie, Ben, and Pax would be going to their home. I knew this was going to be hard, but I could see the value in it. I could see the worth. Jamie and Ben had been courageous in the whole process as any expecting adoptive parents would be.

Although a few times they doubted Lesa would follow through, they held on to hope; this gave me hope. As happy as I was, I was conflicted. I knew this was the right thing, but I also knew the next day would be extremely hard for my daughter. I went to the hospital after I got off work to spend a few hours with Lesa and the baby and told her I would be back to get her tomorrow.

I would have to say the hardest thing I ever had to do was to walk out of the hospital without the baby my daughter had just delivered. A tear fell down my cheek as I tried to keep it together for her. She then placed her hand on my shoulder and the tears became contagious. I knew Jamie and Ben were excited to start their new life, but also knew they felt very strongly for Lesa. They had so much compassion, but it was their day. I saw the goodness although Lesa was crying as the nurse wheeled her out to the car, holding tight to the flowers that Ben had given her for Valentine's Day. The appreciation and love they showed was unexplainable, constantly providing Lesa with affirmation of their joy.

I felt so much pain but, also, so much pride in her decision to do the best thing for her child. Even though Ben and Jamie were excited to have a baby, they felt for her pain. It was both a happy and sad day. As I felt confused in the emotions whirling my mind, what I was witnessing was the most selfless act I have had the pleasure of experiencing in my life; it was also a joyous life-giving gift to a beautiful God-fearing couple. It was a tough day for several different reasons, but I knew God would come through. I was so proud of my daughter, so happy for Jamie and Ben, but my heart ached for her as she climbed into the car then fell down on her knees at the house. I watched as she broke down; I fell down with her, holding her just trying to let her know everything was going to be just as God intended and God always works it out for the good. Witnessing the love of God in my daughter, Jamie, and Ben changed my life; I can never go back.

JaMie

As we left the hospital with Pax and his things all snuggled in, I took a million pictures and texted everyone. We were on our way home (well our friend's) with our first child. Halfway home, I texted Lesa and thanked her. I had so much gratitude for her; I didn't want her to think I was done with her. At the same time it was our time to begin bonding with him.

Immediately after getting to our friend's, Pax was naked; he and I were doing skin on skin while Ben unloaded the car. He then joined us on the bed for our first of many family moments. We lay with him until our friend got home; our first visitors arrived a few hours later. I couldn't stop staring at him, smelling him, and kissing him. Ben and I were addicted. Our guests would hold him and I would die inside waiting to get my hands back on him. God is good to us.

The first night was the most beautiful ever. Pax slept every 2-3 hours, wanted to eat, be changed, and then fall back asleep. It took us a bit to get him situated in his bassinet as I preferred to just hold him. Ben was great too. He was a bit nervous to pat his back to burp him and was trying to get an idea on the most comfortable way to hold him. We took lots of pictures.

That morning, Ben had to work then planned on spending time at our home to work on the water issue. I, on the other hand, had all day with the little guy. Pax slept in his bassinet near the window because he was a little jaundiced. I couldn't get enough; Pax would lie next to me as I took picture after picture while listening to worship music. God was present and more than evident to me. I would send pictures to Ben upon his constant requests. My heart went out to him. He was working so hard and away from his babes.

At about 4:00 in the afternoon I finally heard back from Lesa. I had texted, sent scriptures, and my prayers for her all day. She was hurting but assured me it was what she wanted. The mommy in me wanted to comfort her, but the Lord wanted to do that; He wanted to restore her. So I sent my love and let her know I was available to talk whenever she needed. Ben couldn't have come home fast enough; he wanted his hands on that baby so bad. I remember falling even more in love with him as he held his baby with such pride and gratefulness. He wanted the whole evening with Pax in his arms and me next to him.

We were a family. God was good, but it came with a cost. Jesus paid it years ago; Lesa followed behind, humbling herself and carrying her cross. Her obedience blessed a couple, and the son given to a woman ready to have a baby and a father who was desperate to love a son. She made the decision to deny herself because of her love for her Father and for her son. I'm forever grateful and indebted.

Rosa

Let me just start by saying the God we serve is extraordinary, with the power to give strength to those who are weak, save those who feel they can't be saved, provide grace with no questions asked, and heal seemingly even the most damaged people. There is nothing impossible for our God and once we understand the magnitude of that alone, then we can see how supernaturally, overnight, a heart can heal. Even when that heart seems to have an abundance of scattered, broken pieces, God finds every single piece and molds them back together.

The sun sank and watched the moon pass slowly by. I was excited to see the sun retreat. The darkness connected to my mourning and revealed to me what I was to confront in the shadows: loss, brokenness, confusion, sadness, pain, heartache, stress, and grief. In a jail without bars, I was holding myself prisoner. All these painful things the enemy wanted me to feel were sinking in and tried their hardest to take root. I sulked around the house not wanting to eat, not wanting to be okay. I thought if I was okay, that would make me heartless. I thought if I was going to heal in one day, I was insensitive and would look like I didn't love Paxton. I thought if I was going to smile, I would have been considered lacking compassion.

My spirit wanted to be joyous. I could feel it ready to worship. I didn't understand, "But how God, I don't understand. Why am I supposed to sing songs of praise? How am I supposed to be happy in the midst of my suffering? Shouldn't I be depressed, God?" The answer came quickly. As I sought the LORD, my heart was overflowing with joy and peace. It didn't make sense. Why am I okay? Confused about my afflictions, I laid down, exhausted. I looked at my ceiling and in that moment, God and I began a very intimate conversation.

"God, why do I feel okay?"

"Because you did as I asked."

"But God, How do I know it was You that asked this of me, and not me being selfish? How do I know I did it for you?"

"Do you remember the story of Moses?"

"Yes, God."

"Do you remember why his mother gave him up?"

"To save his life... The Pharaoh was killing baby boys."

"This is true, but there's another reason. This reason alone explains how you know you did it for me.

"What's that?"

"The circumstances that surrounded her were my doing. All the bad was intended for good. It was intended for me. If Pharaoh hadn't been killing baby boys, Moses would never have been placed in the river, and would have never set my people free. So, you see, you got pregnant surrounded by bad circumstances. These circumstances allowed you to give your baby up, in all the bad, because of your obedience, things are going to turn out for the good. This is how you know, you did it for ME."

Shocked at all the information I was receiving, my spirit was still at ease. I thought about Paxton and the amazing things that could come of this. I thought about Ben and Jamie and how they just openly received this gift knowing the possible trials that could come along with it. I wasn't the only one sacrificing. God handpicked Ben and Jamie. He molded the circumstances that surrounded me so Paxton would end up in their home, just like he allowed the river to flow directly to the Queen of Egypt. It was by no accident he closed every avenue I attempted to go down and opened up the one door that would best glorify Him and show His faithfulness to His people.

God doesn't pick something good; He picks the best. I was growing more and more in love with the way God planned our story, I finally felt relieved. I couldn't believe how fast I was healing. I wanted to dance, sing, and just praise Him with all I had!

I got up and turned on my worship music. I choose a remedial song--Where the Healing Begins--I threw my hands in the air and got on my knees. As I cried my eyes out, for the first time since leaving the hospital, these were not tears of sadness, but rather tears of extreme gladness. Tears of hope streamed from my eyes, with a great satisfaction of knowing God had abundantly more for His servant and Paxton would become a great man of God under the authority of a Godly family, chosen just for him. In one night, my open wound of weakness, became a heart strengthened for God, backed up with more than just a bandage. When He puts together the broken pieces of our hearts, He places the Holy Spirit inside before closing the wound; this allows healing not only for a night, but for a lifetime.

"GOD made my life complete
when I placed all the pieces before Him.
When I cleaned up my act,
He gave me a fresh start.
Indeed, I've kept alert to GOD's ways;
I haven't taken God for granted.
Every day I review the ways He works,
I try not to miss a trick.
I feel put back together,
and I'm watching my step.
GOD rewrote the text of my life
when I opened the book of my heart to His eyes." 2
Samuel 22:21-2

Devotion "For God is not unjust,
He will not forget how hard you
have worked for Him and how you have shown your
love to Him by caring for other believers, as you still
do." Hebrews 6:10 NLT

Esther is a great Bible story for any woman. Her
courage, nobility, way with others, and her obedience
for the sake of humanity is so noteworthy and necessary
for believers today. Esther was heralded to be queen
through the favor of God, destined for a position that
would allow access for the saving of many lives.

Skimming through the 8 chapters of Esther would be
beneficial.

Esther became queen because the previous queen
was divorced for not coming to King Xerxes when
called. However, Esther was positioned to come into
the presence of the king without being asked, an equal,

or even worse, offense, than the disrespect Queen Vashti showed. She requested a three day fast, at the end of which she would present herself to the king. Through God's favor she stood before him unscathed; ordinarily those who went before the king without permission were beheaded. In response, the king asks her what he could do for her. She was requesting a pardon for the Jewish people; timing was everything. She could have ignored her uncle's request to ask the king. She could have found herself too caught up in the new culture and consumed with her elevated status to concern herself with others' needs. But she humbled herself even to the point of possible death and chose to stand in the gap for her people. My favorite thought is she is a woman rising to the occasion, the call of true obedience.

"For if you remain silent at this time, relief and deliverance for the Jews will arise from another place, but you and your father's family will perish. And who knows but that you have come to your royal position for such a time as this?" - Esther 4:14 (NIV)

What I think is so imperative to note is that we, as believers, have also come to our royal position for such a time as this.

"But you are a chosen people, a royal priesthood, a holy nation, God's special possession, that you may declare the praises of Him who called you out of darkness into His wonderful light." - 1 Peter 2:9 (NIV)

We must make declarations of praise and draw others out of darkness into His wonderful light.

"You are the light of the world. A town built on a hill cannot be hidden. Neither do people light a lamp and put it under a bowl. Instead they put it on its stand,

and it gives light to everyone in the house. In the same way, let your light shine before others, that they may see your good deeds and glorify your Father in heaven." Matthew 5:14-16 (NIV)

I, Jamie, love how the Message version says it:

"Here's another way to put it: You're here to be light, bringing out the God-colors in the world. God is not a secret to be kept. We're going public with this, as public as a city on a hill. If I make you light-bearers, you don't think I'm going to hide you under a bucket, do you? I'm putting you on a light stand. Now that I've put you there on a hilltop, on a light stand—shine! Keep open house; be generous with your lives. By opening up to others, you'll prompt people to open up with God, this generous Father in heaven."

The purpose of our son's birth - wasn't just that we would finally get a child but rather, that God would be glorified AND that others would be encouraged. The significance of our story isn't the happy ending of becoming parents but rather that we got the chance to see another dimension of God's character...and share that with the world. God is able, mighty and delights in all the details.

"The Lord directs the steps of the godly. He delights in every detail of their lives." Psalm 37:23 (translation)

He is in the details - that He can have the chance to exceed your expectations - to benefit the entire world. Allow God to use your current position, your status, or your situation to use you "for such a time as this" to be a warrior for the cause of advancing His Kingdom.

about the authors

Lesa Childress is a little lady with a big, optimistic, and excited personality. Her heart is found seeking God with all that she is and actively pursuing a P31 lifestyle. Lesa dreams to one day help young girls find their place, purpose, and dreams of their own. She admires the women of her church and knows she has much growing to do, but with coffee and the Word, she feels unstoppable. Lesa was just recently married to Austin Childress and looks forward to a long, loving marriage with the groom God placed in her life

Jamie Ward is the atmosphere director of her home, blogger & is an inspirationalist. Her heart beat is for the orphaned youth of Africa and young adults in her community. Jamie actively serves in her local church & believes every soul matters and is a story to tell. Jamie starts every morning with a nice cup of coffee and ends it snuggled up on the couch with her family. Jamie lives in Republic, Missouri with her groom, Benjamin and her two boys Paxton & Thatcher.

 love connection

21055163R00139

Made in the USA
Charleston, SC
06 August 2013